# WORLD WAR II
## WAR COMES TO AMERICA

# WORLD WAR II
## WAR COMES TO AMERICA

Published by Bookmart Ltd 2005

Blaby Road,
Wigson,
Leicester,
LE18 4SE
Books@bookmart.co.uk

All notations of errors or omissions (author inquiries, permissions) concerning the content of this book should be addressed to TAJ Books 27, Ferndown Gardens, Cobham, Surrey, UK, KT11 2BH, info@tajbooks.com.

ISBN 1-84509-171-X

Printed in China.
1  2  3  4  5  08  07  06  05

# CONTENTS

*Convoys - RCN - Canadian destroyer escorts convoy in British port.*

For the Allies, upon whom Roosevelt had conferred the somewhat grandiose title of "United Nations", 1942 had begun badly in South-East Asia, when the Japanese got within striking range of Australia. But still greater disaster was to strike them in the Atlantic, on the American east coast and in the Caribbean, extending well into 1943. This was, of course, the new U-boat offensive, which between January 1942 and March 1943 would account for 1,673 merchant ships, totalling about 8½ million tons.

On December 8, 1941, with the attack on Pearl Harbor by the Japanese, Hitler had lifted all the efficiency-limiting restrictions which he had imposed on the use of U-boats in the Atlantic. Three days later, the American chargé d'affaires was summoned to the Wilhelmstrasse and handed his passport. Dönitz was now free to fight the "tonnage war" in any way he pleased, with efficiency his only criterion, instead of being confined to those theatres where the counter-measures of the Royal Navy were becoming daily more effective.

At the end of 1941, Dönitz had 249 U-boats available, of which 158 were undergoing trials or training in the Baltic; of the remaining 91 combat U-boats, various postings, at which Dönitz had protested vigorously but which had been ordered directly by the Führer, had deprived him of another 36 (of which 23 were caught in what Dönitz described as the "Mediterranean mousetrap"). Thus only 55 boats were left for duty in the vital Atlantic, a number still further reduced because some were under repair or being overhauled in their bases. Dönitz was left with only about a dozen units for active service in the Atlantic.

From December 9, 1941, therefore, Dönitz decided to unleash Operation "Paukenschlag" ("Kettledrum-roll") against American merchant shipping, to cash in on the latter's inexperience. From January to June, the German raiders, operating singly on the American eastern seaboard, achieved results that can only be compared with those of a pack of wolves let loose among a herd of sheep. Many aspects of World War II remain controversial, but upon this, opinion is unanimous: America was totally unprepared to take part in a ruthless struggle of this nature and her merchant shipping suffered greatly.

The defence of the American east coast from Canada to Florida, was the responsibility of the American Atlantic Fleet, commanded by Admiral R. E. Ingersoll, who took over from Admiral King when the latter became Commander-in-Chief of the United States Fleet. Under his overall authority, the responsibility for the defence of this enormous coastline fell upon Vice-Admiral Adolphus Andrews whose task was to be almost impossible because of this striking material weakness.

## Outmoded command structure

Indeed, the fact is that when war was declared on America, Andrews had under his command only 12 surface vessels, three of which dated from World War I, and 103 aircraft, of which most were unfit for combat duty. Furthermore, whereas the British Admiralty was formally empowered to issue orders to R.A.F. Coastal Command, the same was not true in America, where, by a law dating from 1920, the U.S. Navy had authority only over aircraft of the U.S. Marine Corps and aircraft taken on board a ship, all other land-based aircraft coming under the orders of the Army. Even Churchill, in his memoirs, comments discreetly "… it is remarkable that no plans had been made for coastal convoys and for multiplying small craft."

Churchill's alarm when faced by this situation was perfectly understandable. On February 10 he took the initiative in offering the U.S. Navy ten corvettes and 24 trawlers fitted with the latest asdic.

## America adopts the convoy system

On April 1, the U.S. Navy had at last organised its first convoys along the east coast. But lacking adequate escorts the convoys had to anchor each night in protected harbours, after daily stages of less than 150 miles. Continuous convoys between Halifax, Nova Scotia, and Key West in Florida could not be instituted until the end of May.

Faced with this new situation, Dönitz recalled his U-boats operating off the east coast of the U.S. to the middle of the Atlantic, where they again began to hunt in packs, as before. He had great success in the second quarter of 1942, especially as the number of U-boats under his command was growing. No less than 455 ships, of more than two million tons total displacement, were sunk.

But Dönitz was also a worried man. To replace the 12 U-boats lost in the Atlantic in the first six months of the year, he had received 41 new craft, of which Hitler had taken 26 for the defence of Norway and two for the Mediterranean. On June 17, Dönitz radioed the following question to Lieutenant

Mohr, commander of U-105 and one of Germany's ablest U-boat captains, just as he was attacking a convoy sailing from Nova Scotia: "Have you personally noted the use by the enemy of surface detection apparatus?" Mohr's negative reply was only partially reassuring.

## The "wizard war"

Although he managed to obtain the use of 24 Junkers Ju 88's from the Luftwaffe to counter the activities of Coastal Command, on June 24 Dönitz was forced to order his boats not to surface while passing through the Bay of Biscay except to recharge their batteries. This had the unfortunate consequence for the Germans of greatly reducing their U-boats' operational radius.

Until they could be fitted with radar similar to that fitted to surface vessels, the U-boats were equipped with "Metox" apparatus, which recorded the British radar impulses and could thus tell the U-boats' captains when they had been spotted. But the "Metox" apparatus was designed to receive on the 150-cm wavelength, whereas the British and Americans were in the process of installing new equipment which operated on the 10-cm wavelength. This allowed the Allied anti-submarine patrols to spot the conning tower of a U-boat at a range of up to five miles. Thus, good as the German "Metox" was, it was obsolete by the standards of the improved British radar.

## "Huff-Duff"

The tactic of hunting in packs presupposed a continuous exchange of information between U-boats at sea, and also between

*Germany Kriegsmarine - German submarines refuel at Norway base.*

U-boats and their bases. But the British and Americans were able, however, to take advantage of this from the autumn of 1942 onwards by fitting their escort craft with H/F D/F (High Frequency Direction Finder or "Huff-Duff"), which enabled them to fix the position of a U-boat transmitting, up to a range of 25 miles away. Thus when a U-boat was discovered in the vicinity of a convoy, it was a simple matter to alter course away from the area, while sending in an escort to attack the U-boat. Meanwhile, the convoy, with the rest of the escort, would be steaming away from the place where the pack might be expected.

It was Churchill who described this closely-contested technological conflict as the "wizard war". But the most decisive element in the struggle was to be the air power which the Allies could call into play. On August 21, faced with the constantly increasing number of British and American aircraft now helping in convoy duties, Dönitz noted in his diary:

"The difficulties to be expected from that direction could lead to heavy, even disastrous, losses, to less successful results, and therefore to a lessening of the possibility of success in the submarine war."

*Italian POW's captured by British forces.*

## The Casablanca landings

During the night of November 7, the Western Task Force split into three attack groups and took sub-task forces to positions off the beaches of Safi, Fedala, and Mehdia. Although Patton's objective was Casablanca, the city was too strongly fortified and defended to be taken by frontal assault from the sea. He had therefore divided his troops into three landing forces. Those going ashore at Mehdia were to capture the airport at Salé; the other two forces, after establishing beach-heads, were to converge on Casablanca from the landward side.

Up to virtually the last minute, the surf conditions made landings dubious. But when final readings indicated that the weather might moderate, Hewitt decided to gamble and go. Instead of finding a heavy swell, the troops sailed the last few miles to their beaches in almost a flat calm.

Major-General Lucian Truscott was in charge at Mehdia, with about 9,000 men from the 2nd Armoured and 9th Divisions. With his usual proficiency, he took in hand the members of his force, which had become somewhat disorganised in the initial landings at five different points along the shore. French resistance was immediate and strong, and an air bombardment of the ships offshore at dawn of November 8 delayed and reduced the prompt reinforcement and support that had been planned.

At nightfall of D-day, the Americans were in precarious positions. Hard fighting carried them through the second day. Not until the late afternoon of November 10 was the airfield objective taken and secured. As the battle was about to start again on November 11, word came that a cease-fire had been arranged

General Eisenhower was Commander-in-Chief for Operation "Torch". Eisenhower's H.Q. was run by Major-General Walter Bedell Smith on the basis of allied unity. Major-General George Patton was to lead the American ground forces and General Kenneth Anderson the British forces. Torch was to consist of three major landings: the Western Task Force, to land near Casablanca, was wholly American, sailing from Virginia. The Centre Task Force, to land at Oran, was American but transported from Britain in British ships. The Eastern Task Force, to land near Algiers, would have a token American advance guard to soothe French sensibilities, but was to be predominantly British.

in Algiers.

## Resistance and armistice

The Safi landings were under Major-General Ernest N. Harmon, a cavalry and tank officer who commanded the 2nd Armoured Division. He had a force of about 6,500 men from the 2nd Armoured and 9th Divisions. On the beaches they met strong opposition from the French. But they fought inland and established a beach-head. There had been serious fighting at all three landings of the Western Task Force, the assumption or the hope that the French were anxiously awaiting their liberation by the Allies proving wrong. After three days of combat in Morocco, American casualties totalled about 550, including 150 killed.

## Success at Oran

At Oran, the Centre Task Force, numbering about 22,000 men, was to come ashore in three major operations. In general, the 1st Armoured Division, only about half of which was present, was to thrust inland before daylight and close on the city from the south. The 1st Infantry Division was to encircle the city from the west and east and block the arrival of French reinforcements.

The landings were uniformly successful, although the number of troops ashore at the end of the first day. Arzew was captured intact, as was an airfield. The French naval installations and ships at Oran and Mers-et-Kébir offered weak opposition, and French air efforts were negligible. Only a frontal assault on the Oran harbour and an airborne attack on Tafaraoui airfield miscarried.

The seizure of Oran had been accomplished in less than three

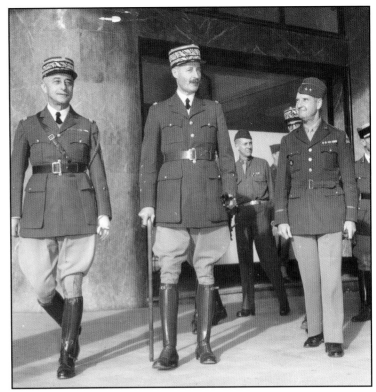

*Generals Giraud and Nogues at French HQ.*

days. Surprise had taken the men ashore without significant French opposition. Sheer determination had carried them inland and to their main objectives rapidly. American casualties totalled about 275 killed, 325 wounded, and 15 missing.

## Algiers, the key

Algiers was the most important objective of "Torch" because it was closest to Tunis, the ultimate goal. In addition, the port, railway terminal, two airfields, space for a supply base, city facilities for headquarters, and the fact that Algiers was the seat of government for all of French North Africa made it a great prize.

The Eastern Naval Task Force divided into three columns,

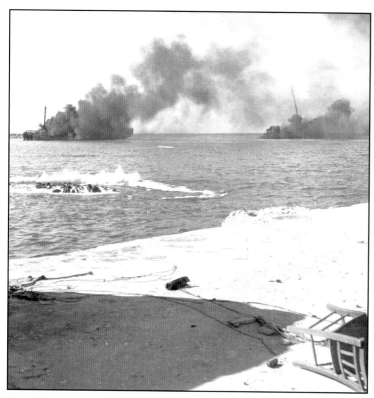

*Bengahazi recaptured.*

one heading for Cape Matifou, two toward Cape Sidi Ferruch. Because there were insufficient Americans for the landings, 7,200 British troops of the 11th Infantry Brigade Group came ashore west of Algiers near Castiglione. The operations went smoothly. French units in the area said they had been instructed not to resist.

Part of the U.S. 34th Division landed closer to the city on its western side. Components were scattered by landing craft along 15 miles of the coast, and all met some French resistance. But the force of 4,350 American and 1,000 British troops took Blida airfield and a small group entered the city.

The 39th Regimental Combat Team, of about 5,700 Americans reinforced by 200 British Commandos, landed

successfully east of Algiers and moved to their assigned positions.

A suicide group of 650 Americans and several British officers in American uniforms made a direct assault on the harbour. By 0800 hours on November 8, they had taken their objectives, an electric power station, a petroleum storage depôt, a seaplane base, port offices, docks, and moles. They were then surrounded by French military units, and had to surrender.

The presence of Darlan in the city was fortuitous. Having to decide whether French North Africa would pass to the Allies with or without bloodshed, he radioed Pétain for instructions and received authority to act freely. Around 1600 hours, with Allied troops closing in on the city, Darlan authorised General Alphonse Juin to negotiate for an armistice in Algiers, but not for all of French North Africa. Two and a half hours later, agreement was reached to halt the fighting.

On the following day, Clark arrived in Algiers to negotiate with Darlan a settlement for the rest of North Africa. They reached agreement late on November 10, and hostilities between the French and the Allies ended.

By then, General Anderson had arrived in Algiers on November 9, and was getting his 1st Army's movement eastward organised and started. Tunis, along with Bizerta, was 380 miles away, and the Axis nations had already started to pour troops into the north-eastern corner of Tunisia by sea and air. French forces offered no resistance, for officers and men were anguished by the conflict between their strong sense of duty to Pétain and Darlan and by their strong desire to join the Allies and fight the Axis. While negotiations took place in Algiers, French officers waited for instructions on whether to collaborate with the Axis or with the Allies. Meanwhile, considerable numbers of German and Italian troops arrived through the ports and airfields of Bizerta and Tunis and established a strong beach-head. Not until mid-November could French ground troops form a thin defensive line to keep the Axis units somewhat bottled up while Anderson's forces rushed to their aid.

Given the distances, the poor roads, and the rough terrain, the Eastern Task Force, predominantly British, made excellent progress. By November 20, Anderson's formations were in contact with Axis units. Five days later, the British, reinforced by a relatively few American units known as Blade Force and by French forces, attacked. But combat strengths on both sides of the front were equal, and Anderson was at a disadvantage. His line of communications was weak, a depôt system was lacking, and air support was difficult to obtain.

Anderson was not to blame. Allied planners had long been aware that the precipitous advance to Tunis on a shoestring would be a gamble. Although Anderson tried for another month to crack the enemy defences, increasingly bad weather, including heavy rains, made it obvious that the Allies could not force a favourable decision before the end of the year.

Eisenhower had done all he could to help. He had sent U.S. units from Algiers and Oran, indeed as far away as Morocco, to reinforce Anderson. He had put pressure on the airmen and logistics experts to give Anderson as much support as possible. But on December 24, after visiting Anderson, Eisenhower had to agree that an immediate attempt to capture Bizerta and Tunis would

have to be abandoned. A stalemate disappointing to the Allies now set in.

This brought "Torch", the landings and the sweep to the east, to an end. The assassination of Admiral Darlan on the same day, December 24, underscored the conclusion of the operation. A new political situation now had to be dealt with. There were also new military conditions. Rommel's forces had been driven from Egypt and across Libya and were about to enter southern Tunisia.

"Torch" represented the first successful major Anglo-American combined offensive, and it set the pattern for Allied unity and cohesion in subsequent coalition ventures. Largely improvised, "Torch" was a triumph of planning and execution, for it required an unprecedented effort to build up an American task force in the United States, separated by 3,000 miles from the other two task forces and from Eisenhower's headquarters, then to arrange for the entire force to converge simultaneously on the North African coast.

*8th Army enters Tripoli in Valentine tanks.*

On February 20, 1943 General Alexander, whose new command had got off to such a bad start, called upon Montgomery to lend a hand in easing the enemy pressure on the British 1st Army. Eager to help, Montgomery, pushed his advanced forces almost as far as the Mareth Line, which General Messe was holding with six Italian and two German divisions. But on February 22, Rommel, leaving the "Centauro" Armoured Division to cope with the American II Corps, had left Thala and dashed south-east with the 10th and 21st Panzer Divisions.

The final plan was not Rommel's but Messe's and Ziegler's. The Italian 1st Army would engage the British head on, whilst an armoured force consisting of the 10th, 15th, and 21st Panzer Divisions, plus the 164th Light Division, would strike from the Matmata mountains and head for Métameur and Medenine, attacking the enemy from the rear, and driving to the Gulf of Gabès. In other words, a repeat performance of Gazala and Alam el Halfa. But this time the three Panzer divisions, with only 141 tanks, were two-thirds below strength, and air support, provided by 160 planes (of which 60 were Bf 109 fighters and 20 Stukas), was very meagre. Neither Messe nor Rommel had any great illusions about the eventual success of their attack, which was due to be launched on March 5.

## Montgomery halts Rommel

Montgomery knew his Rommel well, and at the first hint of an attack, he regrouped his 2nd New Zealand Division, two other infantry brigades, and two armoured brigades, and positioned them on a front all of 43,000 yards long, at right angles to Rommel's expected line of attack. 810 medium, field and anti-tank guns, including many of the brand new 17-pounder anti-tank guns being used in battle for the very first time, lay waiting for the moment to open fire.

Firing a series of concentrated and accurate salvoes at the slightest sign of enemy movement within range, the British artillery forced Rommel to break off contact, with the loss of 52 tanks and 640 men killed, wounded, or missing. The British lost one Sherman tank and 130 men. Montgomery expressly forbade his men to pursue the enemy, who retreated behind the Matmata mountains.

Two days later Rommel left Africa for good, but his departure was kept secret, so as not to jeopardise German morale and encourage the enemy. Colonel-General von Arnim succeeded him as C.-in-C. of Army Group "Africa", and tank specialist General Gustav von Vaerst took command of Pz. A.O.K. 5, Meanwhile, O.K.W. had transferred to North Africa the "Hermann Göring" Panzer Division, the "Manteuffel" Division, and the 999th Division, recruited from among military prisoners, who were thus offered the chance of rehabilitating themselves.

But these reinforcements, which raised the number of divisions under Arnim's command to 16, should not deceive us. A number of the divisions were worn out, and the stubbornness of the two dictators forced them to defend a front nearly 400 miles long. Furthermore,, it was becoming more and more difficult to supply them from Europe.

On February 21, as the battle for Thala was at its height, General Alexander was briefing his commanders on his strategic aims. To destroy the enemy forces engaged in Tunisia, he planned that the necessary operations should be subdivided into two phases: firstly the 8th Army would break through at Gabès and join up with the British 1st Army; then together they would crush the enemy by a careful and overwhelming concentration of land, sea, and air power.

The problem was not so much the size of the forces available, which were increasing week by week, but the time limit it imposed on Alexander. If, as the Casablanca Conference had laid down, the Allies were to land in Sicily during the July full moon, the North African campaign would have to be decided by May 15 at the very latest.

## The Mareth Line

On March 20 at 2230 hours, the 8th Army's artillery opened fire on General Messe's forces: from right to left, i.e. from the Matmata mountains up to the Gulf of Gabès, these comprised the XXI and XX Corps commanded by Generals Berardi and Orlando. Thirty minutes later, the British XXX Corps (Lieutenant-General Oliver Leese) attacked the enemy along its coastal sector.

This frontal attack was to be accompanied by a flanking attack carried out by Lieutenant-General Freyberg's New Zealand Corps which, advancing along the corridor bounded on the left by the Grand Erg and on the right by the Matmata mountains, would take the El Hamma pass, held by General Mannerini's Sahara group, and dash for Gabès, where it could cut the Italian 1st Army's lines of communication; since El Hamma was 120 miles away from Foum-Tatahouine, Freyberg had begun to advance on March 18. His 2nd New Zealand Division was reinforced by the 8th Armoured Brigade and Leclerc's column. Such was the general aim of Operation "Pugilist".

The results, however, fell far short. On the afternoon of the first day, heavy rain had made a quagmire of the Wadi Zigzaou, which flowed in front of the Mareth positions and formed an anti-tank ditch 40 yards wide and 4 yards deep, so that by dawn on March 21, only six of the 50th Royal Tank Regiment's tanks had managed to get through to the opposite side and support Major-General J. S. Nichols's 50th Division, which was having a very bad time under the concentrated fire of the "Giovani Fascisti" Division under General Sozzani. An attempt by the Royal Engineers' bulldozers to breach the bank of the Wadi Zigzaou fared no better. Then the 15th Panzer Division (Major-General Willibald Borowietz), which was being held in reserve, counter-attacked with great vigour: by March 23 the attackers had only one foothold on the left bank.

Instead of using the New Zealand Division in a subsidiary operation Montgomery decided that Freyberg's men would make his main thrust. Whilst the 4th Indian Division under Major-General F.I.S. Tuker was attacking the Matmata range on Messe's flank, X Corps and the 1st Armoured Division (Major-General R. Briggs) had been released in the wake of the 2nd New Zealand Division, and in order to deceive the enemy still further, Major-General G. W. E. J. Erskine's 7th Armoured Division had been brought into the front line. Truth to tell, this ruse did not have as much success as had been hoped for it, for by March 21 General Messe had already got wind of Freyberg's move, and had sent the 164th Light Division and the 21st Panzer Division towards El Hamma.

At 1600 hours on March 26, only 20 minutes after the 1st Armoured Division's last tank had entered the line, Lieutenant-General Horrocks gave the signal for the attack, greatly helped by the sun and a violent sandstorm, which blinded the enemy. The trump card, however, was probably the Desert Air Force, which hurled itself at the defence with devastating effect.

## Messe pulls back

The Allied breakthrough at El Hamma took place too late to enable X Corps to reach Gabès before the bulk of the Italian army could be withdrawn. Whilst the loss of 16 infantry battalions, 31 guns, and 60 tanks was a heavy blow, Messe was nevertheless able to regroup his forces in a very strong position along the Wadi Akarit. Here he had only to defend the narrow eight-mile front that lay between the Gulf of Gabès and the lake of Chott et Djerid, and included three hills standing nearly 1,000 feet above the deep furrow that the wadi's high waters had cut into the plain.

Since, time was of the essence, XXX Corps attacked at midnight on April 5, taking advantage of the darkness of the new moon. To avoid any errors they pushed forward in a single line.

There was a moment of panic and confusion before the defence steadied itself and inflicted heavy losses on Major-General D. N. Wimberley's 51st (Highland) Division, going over itself to the counter-attack as dawn came up. The following day, at about midday, X Corps' tanks entered the fray, and a few hours later Arnim decided to retreat, a decision he stuck to in spite of Messe's opinion that they were not yet beaten. The battle of Mareth–El Hamma had given the Allies 10,000 prisoners, and Wadi Akarit brought in 7,000 more.

Arnim's decision was probably justified, as a result of the threat that was looming up on the Italian 1st Army's right flank. Here the dynamic General Patton had not taken long to instil a new spirit into both officers and men of his new command. On March 17 he captured Gafsa, and straightway pushed forward toward El Guettar, Maknassy, and Sbeïtla. On April 8, on the Gabès–El Guettar road, he joined up with the 8th Army, whilst on his left, the French XIX Corps moved towards the Eastern Dorsale. But neither of them was able to intercept the Italian army as it retreated north towards Enfidaville via Sfax and Sousse.

On April 15, Army Group "Africa" was established along a 135-mile front marked by Cape Serrat, Jefina, Sidi Nsir, Medjez el Bab, Bou Arada, the Djebel Garci mountains, Takrouna, and Enfidaville on the Gulf of Hammamet. To defend this line Arnim had 16 divisions.

On the same day, Patton took leave of II Corps, being ordered to Rabat, where Eisenhower had entrusted him with the organisation of America's share in Operation "Husky". It was therefore his second-in-command, Major-General Omar

*Africa Korps with artillery.*

Bradley, who was given the glittering prize of Bizerta to aim for; besides his four American divisions, he also commanded a French unit consisting of the African Rifle Brigade and the Moroccan mountain troops of Colonel de Monsabert.

At the head of his II Corps, Major-General Bradley showed himself to be as good a tactician in practice as he had been in theory when an instructor at Fort Benning. By manoeuvring on the heights, he got the better of resistance in the Tine Valley and thus, at just the right moment, was able to release his 1st Armoured Division to cut the Tunis–Bizerta railway line at Mateur, on May 5. And on that same day, on his left, the 9th Division (Major-General Manton Eddy) and the African Rifle

*Medium tank 'Sherman'.*

Brigade reached the north shore of Lake Achktel, less than ten miles from Bizerta.

On May 6 General Alexander was to deliver the final blow.

## Operation "Strike"

On April 30, Alexander had detached the 4th Indian Division, the 7th Armoured Division, and the 201st Guards Brigade from the 8th Army, and allocated them to IX Corps, which had taken up a position between Lake Kourzia and the south bank of the Medjerda; with the wounding of Lieutenant-General Crocker at this time, Lieutenant-General Brian Horrocks, who has given us a colourful description of the episode, took over from him at

a moment's notice. To disguise the direction of the attack still more from the enemy, the 1st Armoured Division, operating in the Goubellat area, was reinforced by a large number of dummy tanks. At 0300 hours on the first day of this attack, christened Operation "Strike", IX Corps began to advance on a very narrow front, less than two miles wide; the initial attack would be carried out by the 4th Indian Division and the 4th Division (Major-General J.L.T. Hawksworth); 6th and 7th Armoured Divisions were to form the second wave. Artillery preparation consisted of the concentrated fire of 100 batteries, whose psychological effect on the enemy was increased by the massive intervention of the whole of the Desert Air Force. Under such a battering, the resistance of the 334th Division and the "Hermann Göring" Panzer Division — or rather what was left of them — soon disintegrated. At 0730 hours, General Horrocks told his armoured divisions to head the advance; that evening there was one last skirmish when 20 tanks of the 15th Panzer Division tried to counterattack in the Massicault area.

## Tunis and Bizerta fall to the Allies

In the early afternoon of May 7, the 11th Hussars, forming the advance guard of the 7th Armoured Division, entered Tunis. At the same time, the American 9th Division liberated Bizerta, and the 1st Armoured Division bypassed Ferryville and headed for Protville to meet up with the 7th Armoured Division. This link-up, carried out on May 8, led General von Vaerst, the commander of the Axis 5th Army, to ask Bradley for an armistice. And on the next day, Vaerst surrendered unconditionally. "The fall of Tunis and Bizerta clearly came to the German Command both in Africa and Berlin, as a most severe shock," Alexander wrote. "It was not until the evening of the 8th May that the High Command issued a statement that Africa would now be abandoned and the 'thirty-one thousand Germans and thirty thousand Italians remaining' would be withdrawn by sea. I commented in a report to General Eisenhower that night that the Navy and Air Forces would interfere with this programme, which in any event depended on the enemy holding a firm bridgehead in Cape Bon, and reminded him of Mr Churchill's words in August 1940: 'We are waiting, so are the fishes.'"

Thus fell the Axis' northern stronghold, which according to Arnim's order should have prolonged Axis resistance in Africa. The southern stronghold, which included the Cape Bon peninsula and the Zaghouan mountains, was cut in two by a raid carried out by the 6th Armoured Division, which found the Hamman-Lif pass undefended and on May 10 reached the Gulf of Hammamet in the rear of the Italian army. That same day the British V and the French XIX Corps surrounded the Zaghouan mountains and mopped up the remnants of the Afrika Korps. Having exhausted its ammunition, the "Superga" Division surrendered to the "Oran" Motorised Division (Major-General Boissau) at Sainte Marie du Zit, and in the Zaghouan mountains the "Morocco" Motorised Division finished off the 21st Panzer Division, and forced the Italian XXI Corps to surrender to General Koeltz. However, XX Corps continued to offer valiant resistance to the British 8th Army. When, on the evening of May 12, the 90th Light Division was crushed at Bou Ficha and forced to surrender, the knell of the Axis 1st Army sounded. In the circumstances, at 1935 hours, Mussolini sent a telegram to General Messe: "Cease fire! You are appointed a Marshal of Italy! You and your men have fought the good fight." Arnim was captured by troops of the 4th Indian Division under the command of Major-General "Gertie" Tuker after very heavy fighting.

## "Masters of the North African shores"

The exact number of prisoners taken by the Allies is not known. But on May 25 they held 238,243 unwounded prisoners, including 101,784 Germans, 89,442 Italians and 47,017 of unspecified nationality. Of the once-mighty Axis forces, only 638 soldiers succeeded in reaching Italy, among them Lieutenant-General Alfred Gause, Rommel's former chief-of-staff, Bayerlein, Major-General Josef Schmid, commander of the "Hermann Göring" Panzer Division, and General Sogno, commander of the Italian XXX Corps. The Allies, during this seven months' campaign, had suffered 42,924 killed and wounded. 11,104 lost their lives: 2,156 Frenchmen, 6,233 British and Empire troops and 2,715 Americans.

On May 13, two days earlier than planned at the Casablanca Conference, General Alexander could send the following restrained but joyful telegram to London:

"Sir, It is my duty to report that the Tunisian Campaign is over. All enemy resistance has ceased. We are masters of the North African shores."

*British destroyers dropping depth charges.*

The changing fortunes of the Battle of the Atlantic in 1943, January was relatively favourable to the Allies, as winter storms raged over the North Atlantic; in fact they only lost 50 merchant vessels (261,359 tons) against 106 (419,907 tons) in the same month of the previous year.

West of the Canaries, however, a pack of eight submarines skilfully directed to its rendezvous by Dönitz attacked a convoy of nine tankers heading for North Africa; seven of these were sunk; this was a remarkable feat for which Dönitz duly received General von Arnim's congratulations. In February, Allied losses increased and were slightly over 400,000 tons (73 ships). Nonetheless, between the 4th and 9th of this month, the slow convoy S.C. 118

(63 merchantmen and ten escort vessels) fought off 20 U-boats for four successive nights. A survivor from a previous attack, picked up by U-632, had been criminally indiscreet and drawn the attention of his captors to the convoy: the survivor's remarks caused the loss of several hundreds of his comrades' lives. In fact 13 cargo-boats were sunk at dawn on February 9, but as Grand-Admiral Dönitz stated, the defence was keen. The loss of the 13 cargo vessels was countered by that of three U-boats sunk by the escort vessels. They included U-609 (Lieutenant Rudloff) which was sunk by a depth charge from the French corvette Lobelia (Lieutenant de Morsier). In other engagements, a further 16 U-boats were lost during February; on February 28, for the first time since hostilities began, the number of U-boats lost almost equalled

the number completed by German yards.

In view of this slaughter and the escape, which was often noted, of the convoys from the U-boat onslaught, Dönitz thought for a time that a spy or even a traitor must have penetrated his own staff. The Abwehr conducted a search to locate him, but without success. This was not surprising, as, when they changed course to avoid packs, the British and the Americans relied on the contact signals transmitted by their opponents and picked up by their Huff Duff devices. Huff Duff operators had now had so much experience that they were no longer content only to spy out the enemy, but as they were personally involved in operating the device, they also often managed to identify him. In all, 120 merchant ships and tankers, a total of 693,389 tons, were sunk by German action during March: a serious situation for the Allies.

The U-boats had much less success during April, however. Half the number of merchant ships were destroyed (344,680 tons), for the same number of submarines sunk (15). Moreover, the support groups and escort-carriers began to pursue the enemy more and more closely. The results were clear in May. In that month, at least 47 U-boats were destroyed: 41 were sunk in the North Atlantic, whilst Allied losses fell to below 300,000 tons.

"The situation was changing," wrote Dönitz, acknowledging defeat. "Radar, particularly in aircraft, virtually cancelled out the ability of our submarines to attack on the surface. The previous tactics of our submarines could now no longer be employed in the North Atlantic, a theatre where air reconnaissance was too strong for us. Before using such tactics again, we had to restore our submarines' fighting abilities. I drew my own conclusion

and we evacuated the North Atlantic. On May 24 I ordered the submarines to rendezvous in the area south-west of the Azores, taking all the necessary precautions. We had lost the Battle of the Atlantic."

## Dönitz shifts theatres

The first five months of 1943 had cost the Allies 365 ships (2,001,918 tons); in the following seven, the losses were reduced to 232 (1,218,219 tons). July was the only month in which the tonnage destroyed (365,398 tons) recalled the position in the first six months, but the Germans paid heavily for this.

Thirty-seven U-boats were lost, one per 10,000 tons sunk, whilst in March the proportion had been one to 46,200 tons.

As the British squadrons were reinforced by Coastal Command and supported by U.S. planes, they went over to the offensive in the Bay of Biscay. Dönitz thought he could ward off this threat by fitting quadruple 2-cm cannon on the conning towers of his U-boats. However, he was underestimating the danger of planes which were kept informed by radar and armed with heavy machine guns, rockets, bombs, and depth-charges. His failure to understand the situation cost him 22 U-boats between June 1 and September 1, 1943: he was therefore compelled to order his captains to submerge by day when they passed through these dangerous waters; thus their cruises took considerably longer. At night, when they recharged their batteries, his raiders still had to reckon with the enemy bombers, which were fitted with powerful radar-aimed Leigh searchlights.

In bringing the submarine war to the south-west of the Azores,

*Destroyers patrol the Atlantic protecting convoys from U-Boat attack.*

the Grand-Admiral came up against the American defences.

At the Pentagon (which had just been built), Admiral Ernest J. King had appointed Rear-Admiral Francis Low as deputy chief-of-staff specially entrusted with anti-submarine problems. On receiving his report, King set up a 10th Fleet on the following May 20, which by his decision on that day "was to exercise (under the direct command of COMINCH [C.-in-C. U.S. Fleet]) unity of control over U.S. antisubmarine operations in that part of the Atlantic under U.S. strategic control."

Low therefore only acted by King's delegation, whilst King retained command of the organisation. On the other hand, in contrast with what was happening on the other side of the Atlantic, where Sir Max Horton, C.-in-C. Western Approaches, had ships and marine aircraft, the 10th Fleet in Washington controlled neither boats nor planes. In the action it was directing,

it therefore had to make use of the aircraft and formations of the Atlantic Fleet, to which it was not allowed to give any orders. In spite of its paradoxical situation this organisation worked extremely efficiently from the beginning. In July and August the loss of 35 out of the 60 German submarines sunk in all theatres of war was undoubtedly due to the Americans. In the South Atlantic, where the U.S. 4th Fleet was operating, the groups centred on the escort carriers Core, Santee, Card, and Bogue (under the command respectively of Captains Greer, Fisk, Isbell, and Short) took a prominent and praiseworthy part in this success. The result was that every zone in the South Atlantic was closely watched by long-range four-engined planes or by planes from American aircraft-carriers which were specially deployed to hunt submarines in the central and southern Atlantic. The same strict observation was practised even in the Indian Ocean, although not on such a wide scale. The planes of the two great naval powers therefore took a considerable part in the pursuit of our U-boats, and this continued till the end of hostilities."

Amongst the U-boats destroyed in this sector we may mention some returning from Penang in Malaya, which had valuable cargoes of raw materials.

On October 8, 1943 the agreement between the Portuguese and British Governments granting the British naval and air forces the right to establish a base in the Azores was a new blow for German naval strategy; a few months later, moreover, the Americans were granted the same concession. Thus the "Atlantic gap" was finally closed.

# DEFEAT OF THE U-BOATS

## The balance of losses

On December 31, 1943, the German submarine flotillas consisted of only 168 operational units; there had been 212 on the preceding January 1. During the year they had lost 237 U-boats and their crews. Eight of these were the result of accident, 75 were sunk by the Americans, five by the French, one by the Russians, and the remainder (148) by the Royal Navy and Coastal Command squadrons. As against these losses, we must put the losses of all kinds of Allied merchant vessels in 1943: they amounted to 3,220,137 tons, made up of 597 ships. These figures may appear very large, but they are nevertheless 4,570,560 tons and 1,067 ships less than the figures in 1942. During the same period merchant ships and tankers of about 13 million tons were launched in British, Canadian, and American shipyards. Here again the predominance of the U.S.A. became apparent. Their Liberty ships, which were succeeded by their Victory ships, were built with prefabricated parts by methods recommended by the industrialist Henry Kayser, an organiser of genius; they played a distinguished part in the Allied victory of 1945 and the reconstruction of Western Europe, including Germany and Italy, after the close of hostilities. But in spite of this Dönitz did not give up. He believed that new arms would bring victory in 1944, and in the meantime he counted on forcing the enemy to squander his effort within the bounds of the Atlantic; otherwise the Allies would concentrate their resources even more against the industrial might of the Third Reich.

From January 1 to December 31, 1943, more than 680,000 Allied combatants were disembarked in Great Britain and Northern Ireland by 66 convoys as a part of Operation "Bolero", whilst about 127,000 left the British Isles for Africa, Sicily, and Italy. As a general rule the troops crossed the Atlantic without a convoy on fast liners which managed to elude U-boat ambushes. Using the "hot berth" system (two berths for three soldiers), the Queen Elizabeth and the Queen Mary transported 15,000 men per crossing, whilst the French ship Pasteur accommodated 4,500.

Nevertheless the rations, fighting equipment, vehicles, fuel, and ammunition for these 680,000 men went via the usual convoy route, and most of the bombers for the U.S. 8th Air Force and all the fighters reached Britain by sea. Even if they had crossed the Atlantic by air, or via Iceland, their fuel supply could only have been secured by the use of tankers. For this reason, we may conclude that if the German submarine raiders had not been defeated in 1943, there would have been no Second Front in Western Europe in 1944.

*Ship ablaze in the Atlantic after a U-Boat attack.*

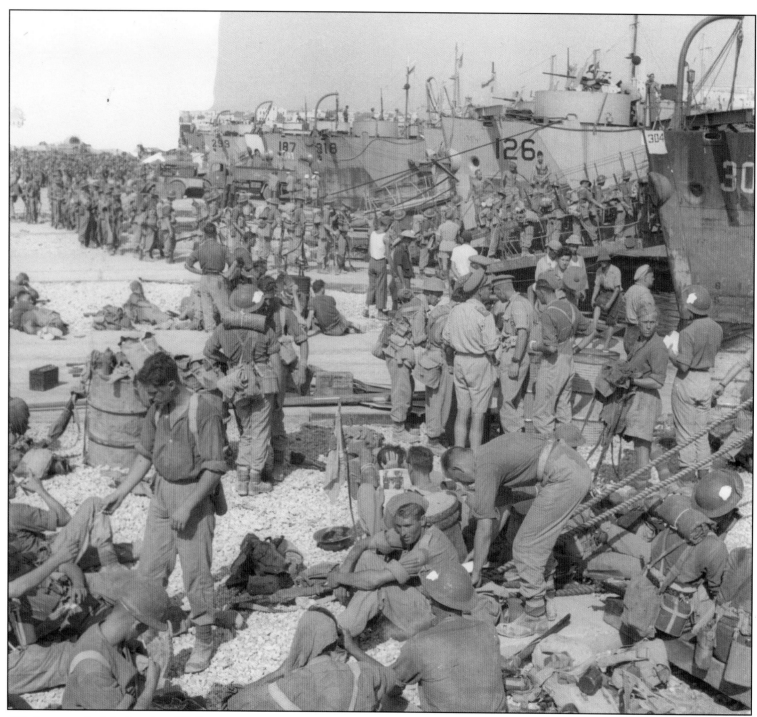

*Allied troops embark for invasion of Sicily.*

After long arguments between the British and the Americans, it was agreed that while an invasion of France in late spring 1944 remained the principal Allied operation against Germany, the Allied forces in the Mediterranean after "Husky" were to mount "such operations as are best calculated to eliminate Italy from the war and to contain the maximum number of German divisions".

For "Husky" General Eisenhower kept the same team which had brought him victory in Tunisia. Under his control General Alexander would direct the operations of the 15th Army Group, the number being the sum of its two constituent armies, the American 7th (Lieutenant-General Patton) and the British 8th (Montgomery): an experienced and able high command.

## Admiral Cunningham's armada

An armada of 2,590 ships, large and small, took part in Operation "Husky" under the command of Admiral Cunningham. Under him Admiral Sir Bertram H. Ramsay was in command of the landings. Ramsay's experience went back to the Dunkirk evacuation, and this time he had 237 merchant vessels and troop transports and 1,742 motorised landing-craft to bring ashore the men, tanks, and supplies. The fighting units had two missions: to neutralise by gun fire all resistance on the shore and to deal with the Italian fleet. They had therefore been given generous support: six battleships, two fleet aircraft-carriers (both British), three monitors, 15 cruisers (five American), 128 destroyers (48 American, six Greek, and three Polish), and 26 submarines (one Dutch and two Polish).

An enormous concentration, but during the first phase of the operation 115,000 British and Canadians and more than 66,000 Americans had to be put ashore.

As for the Allied air forces, they had 4,000 planes under Air Chief-Marshal Tedder. By D-day they had virtually wiped out the enemy's defences. Over Sicily the opposition was a mere 200 Italian and 320 German planes.

At dawn, naval guns and tactical aircraft pounded the Italian coastal defences whilst many landing-craft, loaded with men and tanks, advanced on to their objectives in spite of a choppy sea. D.U.K.W.s, American amphibious trucks, were the first vehicles to land. Franz Kurokowski's monograph on the Sicilian campaign tells of numerous acts of heroism by men of the 206th Division and the 18th Brigade, but faced with companies, battalions, and regiments supported by tanks they were overrun and virtually wiped out. In the evening General Guzzoni ordered the 15th Panzer Division to move towards Enna and the "Hermann Göring" Panzer Division, together with the "Livorno" Division, to mop up the American bridgehead at Gela. In the morning of July 11 the Panzers ran into the forward posts of the 1st American Division in the area of Niscemi but when they had got to within 2,000 yards of the beach they were caught by fire from the cruisers Boise and Savannah and six destroyers, which together loosed off no fewer than 3,194 6- and 5-inch shells at them and wiped out 30 tanks. The "Livorno" Division was also very badly knocked about. On the same day Montgomery occupied, without a shot being fired, the two harbours of Syracuse and Augusta, which had been abandoned by their garrisons in somewhat obscure circumstances.

On July 14 the American 7th Army and the British 8th Army met. This gave them the aerodromes at Ragusa and Comiso, which were put back into shape in record time. Was Montgomery going to race the enemy to Messina and force a surrender, as he had planned? No. Kesselring managed by a great feat to bring over to Sicily two paratroop regiments and the 29th Panzergrenadier Division (Major-General Fries). On July 17 General Hube and the staff of XIV Panzer Corps took command of all German fighting troops in Sicily and resistance stiffened on both sides of Mount Etna. The 8th Army was stopped at Catania and so attacked west of Etna, upsetting the advancing Americans.

Patton, by a miracle of improvisation, then threw his army against Palermo, which fell on July 22, having overcome on the way the "Assietta" Division. He then resumed his advance towards Messina, hoping, like Montgomery, to get there before the Germans. Once again, however, Hube parried and on July 23 the forward units of the American 7th Army were stopped in front of the little town of Santo Stefano on the coastal road. Meanwhile the 1st Canadian Division, which formed Montgomery's left flank, after bypassing the important crossroads at Enna, tried to turn the Etna massif from the north-west.

## Masters of Sicily

Meanwhile the American 9th Division (Major-General Eddy), which had landed at Palermo, and the British 78th Division (Major-General Keightley), now ashore at Syracuse, brought the number of divisions in the 15th Army Group to 11 and gave

the Allies an enormous superiority. Hube therefore began to withdraw, and did it so well that two-thirds of his forces got across to Italy.

Messina and the straits were bristling with A.A., which made life very difficult for Anglo-American aircraft. At 0530 hours on August 17 the commander of XIV Panzer Corps embarked on the last assault-boat leaving for Calabria. Three hours later the Americans and the British were congratulating each other in the ruined streets of Messina.

In his final communiqué, General Alexander announced the capture of 132,000 prisoners, 260 tanks, and 520 guns, and we know from General Faldella, former Chief-of-Staff of the 6th Army, that today there are 4,278 Italian and 4,325 German dead in the war cemeteries in Sicily. On the Allied side, out of 467,000 men in Operation "Husky" the losses were 5,532 killed, 2,869 missing and 14,410 wounded.

*Paratroopers in combat in Sicily.*

*US Army Air Force Spitfire after forced landing on beach at Salerno.*

On July 26 Mussolini was informed by the king that it was his intention to relieve him of his powers and appoint Badoglio as head of the government. Marshal Badoglio's government declared war on Germany on October 13 and received from the "United Nations", as Roosevelt called them, the status of "co-belligerent."

## Near disaster at Salerno

"Salerno: A near disaster" was the title given by General Mark Wayne Clark, commander of the American 5th Army, to the chapter of his memoirs in which he described the landings at Salerno. The whole affair was indeed nearly a disaster and that the

Allies did in fact win through was the result not only of Clark's obstinacy and Montgomery's promptness but also, and perhaps more so, of the bad relationship between Rommel and Kesselring.

The plan drawn up by Generals Eisenhower and Alexander, Air Chief Marshal Tedder, and Admiral Cunningham involved a diversionary action by the 8th Army across the Strait of Messina to pin down the enemy's forces. When this had been done, the 5th Army was to land in the Gulf of Salerno.

On September 3, under cover of fire from a naval force led by Vice-Admiral Willis, and from some 600 8th Army guns the British XIII Corps made a landing on the coast of Calabria north-west of Reggio di Calabria. It met no serious resistance as the 29th Panzergrenadier Division which, with the 26th Panzer Division

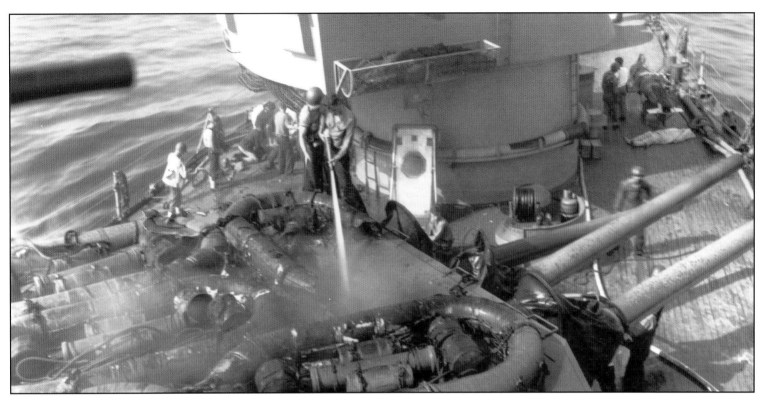

*Warship USS Savanaji, struck by bomb.*

and the 1st Parachute Division, formed the LXXVI Panzer Corps (General Dostler), had received orders not to get caught up in any engagement. General Dempsey thus had no difficulty in pushing his 5th Division up to Pizzo and his 1st Canadian Division to Crotone. This withdrawal by the enemy had not entered into the plans of the Allied 15th Army Group.

Attacked on a front of some 25 miles, the 16th Panzer Division had to give ground but did not disintegrate. By the end of the day the American 36th Division had got five miles inland, but the British X Corps had not reached all its objectives and fighting continued in the streets of Salerno. Sieckenius still controlled the high ground which overlooked the coastal strip from a distance of 600 to 1000 yards. The American 45th Division was landed and this allowed Clark to extend and deepen his bridgehead, which on September 11 was 11 miles inland at its furthest point and stretched from Agropoli to Amalfi with a circumference of over 43 miles.

"Avalanche" was off to a good start. In Frascati, however, Kesselring had remained calm and XIV Panzer Corps was ordered to concentrate and counterattack. LXXVI Corps also came to the rescue, leaving Montgomery facing only its 1st Parachute Division and part of the 26th Panzer Division. The capture of Rome enabled Kesselring to give the 3rd Panzergrenadier Division (Lieutenant-General Graeser) to the 10th Army, so that by September 12 Vietinghoff had five and a half divisions, admittedly understrength, against his enemy's four, scattered over a wide front. This led to a crisis that did not end until September 15.

Profiting from the fact that the British right flank (56th Division) had made slower progress than the American left (45th Division), the Germans attempted to get a pincer movement round the latter, cut the British off from the Americans, and destroy both piecemeal. The crux of this battle was at Ponte Bruciato, where Clark threw in everything he had, including two artillery battalions, a regimental band, and his H.Q. orderlies and cooks. The German advance was slowed down and eventually stopped some five miles from the beach, where it was pinned down by the concentrated fire of the fleet which Admiral Hewitt had brought as close inshore as possible. Although the capture of Rome by the Germans had freed the 3rd Panzergrenadier Division for Kesselring, it also released the American 82nd Parachute Division (Major-General Ridgway) which was to have landed in support of the Italians; during the night of September 13–14 a first paratroop regiment reached the bridgehead.

The final defeat of the German 10th Army at Salerno and the threat to his rear forced Kesselring to disengage on September 16, but this brought a renewed conflict with Rommel, who wanted to abandon Rome, whereas Kesselring maintained that the Eternal City could be covered from a line running roughly Formia-Cassino-Pescara, using the Garigliano and the Rapido valleys and the Abruzzi mountains, which reached over 9,000 feet at La Malella. On November 21 Hitler recalled Rommel and moved Kesselring from his position as C.-in-C. South to head a new Army Group "C", thus leaving him in complete command in Italy.

Hitler transferred the 24th Panzer Division and the S.S. "Leibstandarte" Division to the Eastern Front. Kesselring allotted three divisions to the 10th Army and the balance of Army Group "B" in northern Italy went to form a new 14th Army under General von Mackensen.

## Careful retreat

Meanwhile Vietinghoff, turning to great advantage the demolition and destruction which had been caused and the heavy autumn rains which, according to Montgomery, covered the roads in "chocolate sauce", did not allow his forces to get caught anywhere, either at Termoli on October 4, in spite of a commando landing behind his left flank, or on the Sangro on November 27 when the three divisions and an armoured brigade of V Corps broke out of the bridgehead and advanced along the line Sulmona–Avezzano to wipe out his 65th Division (Lieutenant-General von Ziehlberg). The rubble left after artillery shelling and aerial bombardment by the British, which their own tanks then had to get through (a sight which was to recur in the Caen campaign) made any exploitation impossible and in a couple of days Vietinghoff was making a stand again and stopping the Allied advance.

On December 24 Generals Eisenhower, Montgomery, and Spaatz flew to London and the Italian theatre of operations was relegated to the background.

*Allies use 4.2 inch mortar.*

The breakout from Anzio stalled on the Gothic Line and the initial attacks on Monte Cassino were unsuccessful. General Juin of the French Expeditionary Corps set out a plan on April 4 in a memorandum to General Clark. In his opinion, instead of turning right as soon as Monte Majo had been captured, "they should infiltrate under cover of surprise into the massif dominated by the Petrella and seize the key points… and, from there, by an outflanking movement, open the way to frontal advances mounted concurrently to secure Highway 7 and the road from Esperia up to and including the road running parallel to the front of Arce.

"The aim being to bring to bear on the Arce sector a force of considerable size so as to be able to break out in strength behind the enemy's rear and advance towards Rome."

After a little hesitation Clark was won over to his subordinate's plan. This had the great advantage of including in the French Expeditionary Corps' outflanking movement the Hitler Line or "Senger defile", which blocked off the Liri valley at Pontecorvo. On the other hand there was a formidable obstacle in the Monti Aurunci, which reached over 5,000 feet at Monte Petrella. It might be assumed that the enemy had not occupied the heights in strength, and that surprise could be achieved by using the natural features as Guderian had done in the Ardennes in May 1940 and List in the Strumitsa gap on April 6, 1941.

However, everything depended on the speed with which an early success could be exploited. As usual, Kesselring would not take long to muster his forces, but General Juin was relying on the legs of his Moroccan mountain troops and of his 4,000 mules.

Though Clark agreed to the French plan, he could not get Sir Oliver Leese to accept its corollary, the Atina plan, and though he used a corps against Cassino where Freyberg had sent in one division, the pincer was still too short and there were heavy losses.

Kesselring had 23 divisions, but most of them were worn out and short of ammunition, whereas the Allies had an abundance of everything. Here again the Germans were waging "a poor man's war" as General Westphal put it.

Another serious disadvantage for Kesselring was his enemy's overwhelming superiority in the air and at sea. This was so important that it caused him to worry not only about a landing at Civitavecchia or at Leghorn but also about whether Allied air power would cut off XIV Panzer Corps' communications at Frosinone. The uncertainty of his situation compelled Kesselring to write in his memoirs about his main reason for concern at this time: "The great dangerous unknown quantity which lasted until D-day plus 4 was the following: where would the French Expeditionary Corps be engaged, what would be its main line of advance and its composition?"

## The French go in

At 2300 hours on May 11, 600 Allied batteries (2,400 guns ranging from 25-pounders to 9.4-inch) opened up simultaneously on a front of some 25 miles. At midnight the Allied infantry moved forward. When dawn broke both General Leese and General Clark had to admit that in spite of the surprise effect the night attack had not brought the expected success. The Polish II Corps (General Wladislas Anders: 3rd "Kressowa" and

*Cisterna - reduced to ruins by the fighting in Italy, June 1944.*

*Knocked-out American tank amid ruins of Cassino, Italy, 17 March 1944.*

5th "Carpathian" Divisions) had failed on the slopes of Monte Cassino and, for all the fighting spirit shown by these men, escapees from Russian jails, their losses were very heavy. In the Liri valley the British XIII Corps (Lieutenant-General Kirkman) had got two of its divisions across the Rapido, but without really denting the resistance put up by LI Mountain Corps (General Feuerstein) and here again 1st Parachute Division was particularly successful.

Though the French Expeditionary Corps had been strengthened by the 4th Moroccan Mountain Division (General

Sévez) and the 1st Motorised Infantry Division (General Brosset) its task was not made any easier by the fact that the enemy opposite (71st Division: Lieutenant-General Raapke) was ready and expecting to be attacked. During this night operation, which they were ordered to carry out so as to facilitate the British XIII Corps' crossing of the Rapido, the French stumbled on to minefields and were attacked by flame-throwers. By the end of the day on the 12th it was feared that the French attack might have run out of steam and that Kesselring would have time to occupy the whole of the Petrella massif. Without losing a minute, General Juin reshaped his artillery attack so as to concentrate everything on the Monte Majo bastion. This bold stroke broke the resistance of the German 71st Division and in the afternoon of May 13 the Moroccan 2nd Division raised an immense tricolour on the top of the 3,000-foot hill. On its right the 1st Moroccan Motorised Infantry Division had cleared out the bend in the Garigliano. On its left the 3rd Algerian Division had captured Castelforte and was moving forward towards Ausonia.

## The French push round the east flank

Further over to the left the American II Corps was well on its way to Formia. On that day, as Marshal Juin wrote, "having toured the fronts in the lower areas from end to end of the bridgehead where the actions were developed, I was able to see with what ardour and enthusiasm the troops drove forward to their objectives. It is true that the commanders were there in the breach in person: Brosset, driving his own jeep, was giving orders through a loud-hailer and Montsabert was conducting his battle by means of a portable radio which never left his side. There were also other reasons for this feverish excitement. Towards mid-day a message was heard in clear from the enemy ordering his troops to withdraw and the prisoners were flowing in."

Without losing a moment General Juin threw his Mountain Corps into the breach. This now included the 4th Moroccan Mountain Division and General Guillaume's Moroccan Tabors. Leaving the beaten tracks, with their machine guns and mortars on their backs, they scaled the steep slopes of Monte Petrella like mountain goats, reaching the top on May 15. Without waiting to get their breath back they then hurled themselves at the Revole

massif (4,150 feet). Meanwhile, passing behind the Mountain Corps, the 3rd Algerian Division took Ausonia and reached Esperia, thus extending the action of the 1st Moroccan Motorised Infantry Division which had captured San Giorgio on the right bank of the Liri.

## Poles, British, and Americans drive forward

What would have happened if at the same time the British 8th Army, in a sweep as wide as General Juin had wanted, had outflanked the Pontecorvo position? In all evidence XIV Panzer Corps would have faced total disaster, a disaster which would then have overtaken the 10th Army. It was only on May 17 that the Polish II Corps, now attacking again, found the monastery on Monte Cassino deserted. It was again only on May 19 that the British 78th Division (XIII Corps) attacked the "Senger defile" in the Aquino area, but unsuccessfully. This lack of liaison between the French and the British held up the French Expeditionary Corps' exploitation towards Pico and the Monti Ausoni.

But Kesselring, throwing in everything he could lay hands on, sent units of the 90th Panzergrenadier, the 305th, and the 26th Panzer Divisions to stop them. He also sent the 29th Panzergrenadier Division against the American II Corps, which had advanced through Formia and Itri and by May 22 was threatening Terracina. This was trying to pay Paul by robbing Peter, that is to say Colonel-General von Mackensen. Reinforced to the equivalent of eight. divisions by the transfer of the American 36th Division to the Anzio bridgehead, the American VI Corps had no particular difficulty in breaking the resistance of the German 14th Army during the day of May 23. Forty-eight hours later II and VI Corps met on the shores of Lake Fogliano. On the same May 23 the French Expeditionary Corps was spreading out over the Monti Ausoni whilst the Canadian I Corps (Lieutenant-General E. L. M. Burns: 1st Infantry and 5th Armoured Divisions), which had just relieved the British XIII Corps, was forcing its way through the Pontecorvo defile.

## Kesselring attempts to cover Rome

Kesselring tried once more to protect Rome by establishing a new position on the line Colli Laziali–Monti Lepini to secure Vietinghoff's right, and to achieve this he withdrew from the Leghorn area his last reserve motorised division, the "Hermann Göring" Panzer Division, and sent it immediately to Valmontone. The bombing by the Anglo-American air force, which on one single day (May 26) destroyed 665 vehicles of the 14th Army alone, considerably held up these troop movements. Now Valmontone was, in accordance with General Alexander's instructions, precisely the objective of the American VI Corps. If Truscott, now in Cisterna, therefore advanced with the main body of his forces along the Corti–Artena axis, he had every chance of cutting off the 10th Army's move to cover Rome. The latter's rearguard was still at Ceprano, some 40 miles or more from Valmontone, and the Germans would thus be driven back against the Abruzzi mountains, which were virtually impassable, and entirely cut off.

But, for reasons which Alexander said were inexplicable, Clark ordered VI Corps to attack with its 34th, 45th Infantry,

and 1st Armoured Divisions north west to the line Velletri–Colli Laziali, sending only a slightly reinforced 3rd Division along the Valmontone axis (northwards). This decision, taken in the afternoon of May 25, brought only a slight reaction from Alexander, who remarked to General Gruenther, the American 5th Army chief-of-staff, when the latter brought him the news: "I am sure that the army commander will continue to push toward Valmontone, won't he?"

"Rome the great prize" was the title General Mark Clark gave to the 15th chapter of his memoirs. We are thus forced to conclude that this able but impetuous man had lost sight of the fact that a commander's supreme reward is to receive in his tent those who have been sent on behalf of the enemy commander to sue for conditions of surrender. But Alexander was also taken in by the Roman mirage at this time: did he not forbid the French Expeditionary Corps, then coming down from the Monti Lepini, to use the Frosinone–Rome highway, which he intended to restrict to the British 8th Army?

On May 31 its 36th Division found a gap in the German 14th Army defences, turned the Velletri position and scaled the Colli Laziali. Furious at this setback, Kesselring recalled Mackensen and replaced him with General Lemelsen. He now had to order the evacuation of Rome, which he proclaimed an "open city". On June 4 the American 88th Division (Major-General J. E. Sloan) was the first unit to enter the Eternal City.

General Clark tells a story worthy of inclusion in any history of the campaign. Writing of his first visit to Rome he says:

"Many Romans seemed to be on the verge of hysteria in

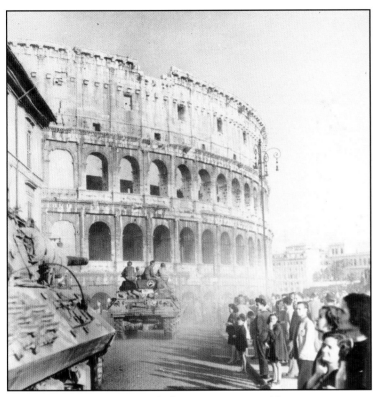

*Rome's population cheers arrival of US troops, June 1944.*

adamant that Operation "Dragoon" (formerly "Anvil"), the landing in the south of France, must now take precedence over any other operations in the Mediterranean theatre now that "Overlord" had taken place, and all effort had to be concentrated.

Marshall, it would appear, was merely obeying the dictates of high strategy. It was clear to him, in effect, that an Anglo-American drive towards Vienna, and out of line with the main thrust, would contribute less to the success of Operation "Overlord" than would a landing in Provence, which would open up the ports of Marseilles and Toulon to Allied men and matériel, whilst a strong Franco-American force, operating first up the Rhône, then the Saône, would give a right wing to Eisenhower when he broke out into Champagne. To him this reasoning respected the principle of the convergence of effort, so dear to American military doctrine. It can easily be seen how Marshall froze at Churchill's passionate arguments.

In any case, it is highly doubtful on military grounds whether an advance to the Alps or into Yugoslavia in 1944 was practicable, even if Alexander's armies had not been weakened for the sake of "Dragoon". The German commanders had proved themselves masters of defensive warfare in mountain regions, and they were to continue giving the Allies immense problems even when operating with minimal resources and under pressure from all sides.

their enthusiasm for the American troops. The Americans were enthusiastic too, and kept looking for ancient landmarks that they had read about in their history books. It was on that day that a doughboy made the classic remark of the Italian campaign when he took a long look at the ruins of the old Colosseum, whistled softly, and said, 'Geez, I didn't know our bombers had done that much damage in Rome!'"

## The agreed strategy is confirmed

However, not even the British Chiefs-of-Staff believed that an advance to the Alps and beyond that year was practical, while President Roosevelt and the American Chiefs-of-Staff remained

*Von Runstedt inspects troops on Channel Coast.*

On D-Day, Rundstedt, as Commander-in-Chief in the West, had the following under his command: two army groups ("B" and "G"), comprising four armies (7th, 15th, 1st, and 19th). These in turn had 15 corps between them, totalling 40 infantry, four parachute, four Luftwaffe field, nine Panzer, and one Panzergrenadier divisions.

However, for all this it is by no means true that Rundstedt exercised over this force the authority normally given to a commander-in-chief. In the first place, the Luftwaffe units (one corps, eight divisions) were only under his tactical command; the same was true of his four Waffen-S.S. divisions and the I S.S. Panzer Corps. He had no authority over these units in the questions of training, promotions, the appointment of commanders or in the field of discipline. That is what Hitler cruelly reminded Rommel, who had requested that action be taken against the 2nd "Das Reich" Panzer Division of the Waffen-S.S., after the appalling massacre at Oradour-sur-Glâne.

Even more, O.B.W. had had it made quite clear that it could not, without the Führer's permission, move two of its best armoured divisions, the 12th "Hitler-jugend" Waffen-S.S. Panzer Division, stationed near Lisieux, and the 130th Panzer-"Lehr" Division, formed the previous winter from Panzer instructors and now stationed around Châteaudun.

A major part of the success of the landings can be explained by the inefficiency of the German Intelligence services. Here the Nazis Kaltenbrunner and Schellenberg, who had ousted the professionals Canaris and Oster, could neither get a clear idea of the British and American plans nor escape being deceived by the Allies' diversionary manoeuvres.

Hitler had given a long analysis on the situation on March 20. Though he recognised that there was no way of being sure in which area the Allies would land, over the whole coastline from Norway to Greece, he nevertheless made his point:

"At no place along our long front is a landing impossible, except perhaps where the coast is broken by cliffs. The most suitable and hence the most threatened areas are the two west coast peninsulas, Cherbourg and Brest, which are very tempting and offer the best possibilities for the formation of a bridgehead, which would then be enlarged systematically by the use of air forces and heavy weapons of all kinds."

This hypothesis was perfectly logical and the order of battle of the German 7th Army (Colonel-General Dollmann), was correctly arranged to face this possibility. Of its 14 divisions, 12 were deployed between the Rivers Vire and Loire.

Rundstedt did not share Hitler's opinion, and considered that there were a great many more advantages from the Allied point of view for them to cross the Channel and land in the Pas-de-Calais. But this would have meant coming up against the strongest part of the Atlantic Wall, whose concrete-housed batteries on either side of Cape Gris-Nez kept the English coast between Ramsgate and Dungeness under the fire of their 14 11-, 12-, 15-, and 16-inch guns; also Colonel-General von Salmuth's 15th Army was well deployed in the area, with 18 divisions between Antwerp

and Cabourg. These troops were of good quality, and so it would seem that at O.K.W. Field-Marshal Keitel and Generals Jodl and Warlimont expected a landing between the mouths of the Rivers Somme and Seine, outside the range of the heavy artillery mentioned above but still within the 15th Army's sector, under the overall command of Field-Marshal Rommel.

## Problems for Coastal Defence

Rommel commanded Army Group "B", which included the 7th and 15th Armies and LXXXVIII Corps, with three divisions for the defence of Holland. His main worry was the weakness of the defences on the beaches of the bay of the Seine, where three divisions were thinly stretched between Cabourg (exclusive) and the port of Cherbourg. More important, this weakness was not compensated for by the density or heavy calibre of the coastal artillery. Actually, on the 125mile front between Le Havre and Cape Barfleur, the Swedish coastal artillery expert Colonel Stjernfelt has identified only 18 batteries, 12 of which could not reach the Calvados beaches or did not fire at all on D-Day.

Another concern of Rommel's was what form he should give to this defensive battle for which he was responsible and which might begin any day. But on this question, his point of view was almost exactly the same as the Führer's, detailed previously.

In his opinion, a sea-borne landing differs from a ground attack essentially in that the latter has its maximum force on the first day of the offensive. It then decreases in momentum because of the losses that are suffered and logistic difficulties. This allows the defending army to put off its counter-attack. On the other

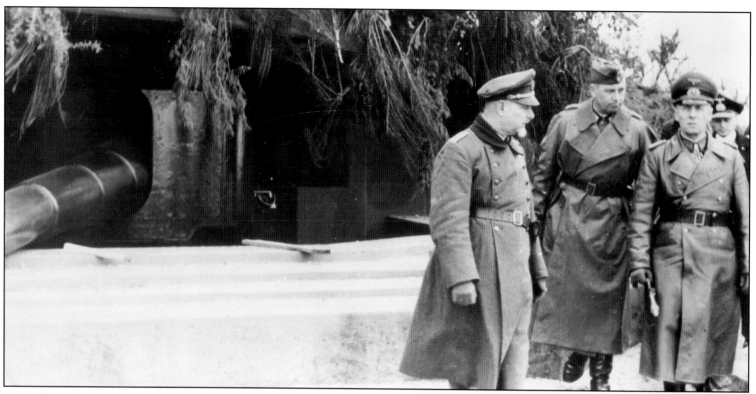

*Rommel inspects Atlantic Wall.*

hand, the enemy who comes from the sea will be weak at the moment of landing, but will become steadily stronger within his bridgehead, so that any delay at all in the counter-attack will reduce in like proportion its chance of success.

The Panzers were indubitably the best means of counter-attack, and so the sensible thing was to deploy them in such a manner that they could be hurled against the enemy wherever he might appear (Low Countries, Pas-de-Calais, Normandy, or Brittany) on the actual day of the landing.

And, in fact, after the conference of March 20, Rommel had received from the Führer the right to have Panzergruppe "West" put immediately under his direct command. This force, under

General Geyr von Schweppenburg, constituted Rundstedt's armoured reserve. But no order had come from O.K.W. to give executive force to Hitler's concession. And so Schweppenburg refused the rôle which Rommel allotted to him. His view was that the Western Front's armoured reserve should be concentrated in a central position downstream from Paris, so that it could intervene with all its strength in that sector where it looked as if the enemy was about to make his main push, after all tricks and feinting movements had been discounted. From this point of view, the way that Army Group "B" at la Roche-Guyon wanted to distribute the Panzers seemed to fit the verdict that Frederick the Great had proclaimed against all systems of wide-stretched defence: "Wer alles defendieren will, defendiert gar nichts" (He who tries to defend everything, defends nothing).

Rundstedt, and also Colonel-General Guderian, agreed with this point of view, which could clearly be defended on the principles of war. But were they applicable in those circumstances? Rommel denied that they were and cited as an example, as has been seen, his North African experience. His opponents had not had this experience as they had all come from the Eastern Front, where the enemy's tactical air force was only just beginning to show its power to paralyse ground movement. Events showed that his reasoning was without doubt the more pertinent. However that may be and in spite of his attempt on April 23, Rommel received no satisfaction on this vital point. Better — or worse still — depending on one's point of view, the Führer was equally negative when Rommel suggested that he should advance the Panzer-"Lehr" Division to between the Orne and the Vire, deploy the "Hitlerjugend" Division in the region of Saint-Lô, and reinforce this sector, which seemed dangerously weak to Rommel, by a brigade of Nebelwerfers (976 15-, 21-, and 30-cm barrels) and a large number of heavy (8.8-cm) anti-aircraft batteries. Faced with silence from Hitler, Rommel left la Roche-Guyon at dawn on June 4 for Berchtesgaden, not without having consulted his barometer and obtained Rundstedt's leave.

In spite of the documents published since 1945, Hitler's attitude when faced with the problems of the German high command remains incomprehensible, for it abounds in contradictions. The facts speak for themselves.

Though he did not believe the forecasts of his subordinates at O.K.W. and of Rundstedt, all of whom envisaged the British and

*Czech Howitzer is prepared for firing, Atlantic Wall.*

the Americans approaching the French coast between Le Havre and the Pas-de-Calais, he accepted their forecast the day after the Allies landed in the bay of the Seine and stuck to it obstinately until a decisive hole was punched in the German line on the left bank of the Vire by the 1st American Army. In fact he was convinced, up to July 24, that the only purpose of the Battle of Normandy was to trick him into lowering his guard in the Pas-de-Calais. Here he too was deceived by the Allied cover plan, which continued to give the impression that there were powerful forces in south-east England about to attack directly across the Channel in the Pas-de-Calais.

However, though his hypothesis of March 20, concerning the first objectives of the Allied attack, only partially " coincided with Rommel's views, in other respects there was perfect agreement between the two men concerning the way to repel it: an immediate counterattack on the beaches so as to avoid a long battle of attrition, like the one the armies had fought at Anzio–Nettuno.

When one reviews the first 24 hours of Operation "Overlord", the rôle of the Resistance must first be mentioned. It was in fact vital. No military operation was ever based on such comprehensive Intelligence as "Overlord". Evidence for this is offered by the remarks of the operations officer of the 12th "Hitlerjugend" S.S. Panzer Division when he examined a map which had been found on June 8 in the wreck of a Canadian tank. "We were astounded at the accuracy with which all the German fortifications were marked in."

## Weather conditions against the Allies

It is well known that weather conditions played an important part in the way that the Germans were taken by surprise at dawn on June 6. They had a paralysing effect. Rommel's opinion, that the landing would only take place when dawn and high tide coincided, was also mistaken. Up to now the weather conditions had favoured the Allies. After midnight on June 5, the weather turned against them; although the wind had fallen a little, as Group-Captain Stagg had predicted, it was blowing strongly enough to scatter widely the paratroopers of the 82nd and 101st American Airborne Divisions, who had dropped over the Cotentin peninsula, and the British 6th Airborne Division which had dropped between the Orne and the Dives.

A few hours later, the bomber attack failed for the same reason to neutralise the "Omaha" Beach defences. In the same sector, disaster met the amphibious tank formation which was to support the left wing of the American 1st Division: of the 32 tanks which were launched into the water 6,000 yards from the shore, 27 sank like stones with most of their crews; the canvas flotation skirt supported by a tubular framework gave the tanks only about 3 feet free-board-but the sea was running with a swell of more than 3 feet. The Americans who landed between Vierville and Saint Laurent were therefore put to a gruelling test.

## Allied air supremacy all important

Admiral Sir Bertram Ramsay, the commander of the naval Operation "Fortune" supporting "Overlord", is said to have likened the invasion army to a shell fired by the navy, but Montgomery asserted that only air supremacy would ensure naval supremacy.

On June 6, 1944, the Anglo-American forces conformed to the two conditions laid down by the two British war leaders. In the air General Eisenhower, faced with 419 Luftwaffe planes, had more than 10,500 fighting planes at his disposal: 3,467 four-engined bombers; 1,645 twin-engined bombers; and 5,409 fighter bombers and interceptor fighters. Therefore he was in a position to use 2,355 transport planes and 867 gliders carrying about 27,000 troops and their matériel including light tanks, with no risk of attack by German fighters, though there was still the threat of anti-aircraft defences.

## The Allied invasion fleet

At sea, the embarkation fleet from British ports consisted of 5,339 ships and was in the Channel on Sunday June 4 when it received the signal that the assault was deferred from the following day to June 6; a part of the fleet spent the day cruising in the area.

*Normandy, landing supplies for allied forces.*

But the bad weather which caused the postponement also kept the Luftwaffe patrols grounded; otherwise they would have spotted and reported this unusual concentration of ships. On the evening of June 5 the fleet assembled south of the Isle of Wight and made for its objectives in ten columns.

Admiral Ramsay had divided his forces into two:

1. Under the American Rear-Admiral A. G. Kirk, the Western Naval Task Force was to land and support the American V and VII Corps on the "Utah" and "Omaha" Beaches on both sides of the Vire estuary. All ships flying the Stars and Stripes, including the Nevada, a survivor from Pearl Harbor, had appropriately been assigned to him.

2. Under Rear-Admiral Sir Philip Vian, the Eastern Naval Task Force was to perform identical services for the British I and XXX Corps which were to come ashore between Ver-Plage and Ouistreham on the beaches called (from west to east), "Gold", "Juno", and "Sword".

When reviewing the Allied air and naval forces, the power and quality of the support they gave the land forces in the hard fighting against the defenders of the Atlantic Wall must be emphasised. For example, two of the three Czechoslovak 8-inch guns comprising the Saint Marcouf battery had been destroyed; similarly the four 6-inch guns of the Longues battery, near Port-en-Bessin, were silenced by the fire of the cruisers Ajax, Montcalm, and Georges Leygues. In addition, Allied air forces over the battle sector had been increased and they responded rapidly, accurately and efficiently to all requests from the ground forces. From dawn to dusk they had made over 4,600 sorties, while only about 50 planes reminded both sides of the Luftwaffe's existence.

The Germans guarding the coast on the night of June 5–6 were frequently caught off their guard: in Paris and in Rastenburg the news was received sceptically. 'What, in this weather?' Even the chief-of-staff C.-in-C. West scoffed: 'Maybe a flock of seagulls?''

At the end of the first day, Eisenhower and Montgomery were in a position to make the following estimate of their gains:

On the whole, the landing had been successful, but the Americans and the British had nowhere gained their prescribed objectives for the evening of D-Day. North of the Vire the American 82nd and 101st Airborne Divisions, under Major-Generals M. B. Ridgway and M. D. Taylor respectively, which were due to protect VII Corps' right (Lieutenant-General J. L. Collins) and give it access to the right bank of the Merderet, had scattered in small pockets in the night; in addition they lost many men and much matériel in the shallow floods and minefields laid by the Germans. In short, of the 17,262 fighting men of the two divisions who jumped or landed on "the longest day", 2,499, or nearly 15 per cent, were missing.

Nevertheless a regiment from the 82nd Airborne Division had occupied the small town of Sainte Mère-Eglise (because of the panic flight of a service unit of German A.A. defences), maintained its ground, and in the evening had made contact with the American 4th Division which had landed on "Utah" Beach. This unit under Major-General Barton had had a relatively easy task, as the air and naval bombardment on the support points of the German 709th Division (Lieutenant-General von Schlieben) barring its way had been completely and devastatingly effective.

## Omaha Beach

When it landed at "Omaha", the American 1st Division (Major-General C. R. Huebner) had been given the main road N.13, which runs from Caen to Cherbourg, as its objective for the day. This required an advance of three miles from the Vierville beach. It was also to extend its right as far as Isigny and its left as far as the western approach to Bayeux, where it was to make contact with the inner flank of the British 2nd Army. For this purpose Major-General L. T. Gerow, commander of V Corps, had reinforced his corps with a combined regiment drawn from the 29th Division. At nightfall the 1st Division had not got beyond the small villages of Saint Laurent and Colleville.

In addition the air bombardment had missed its target, the majority of the D.D. tanks had sunk before they reached the beaches, and the 1st Division had come up against the newly-arrived, elite 352nd Division. Although U.S. Command knew of this development they had failed to inform their combat troops. At about 1000 hours General Bradley, the commander of the American 1st Army, had sent ashore his chief-of-staff and received a discouraging report from him:

"The 1st Division lay pinned down behind the sea wall while the enemy swept the beaches with small-arms fire. Artillery

*Troops prepare to land, Omaha Beach, Normandy, 7 June 1944.*

chased the landing craft where they milled offshore. Much of the difficulty had been caused by the underwater obstructions. Not only had the demolition teams suffered paralysing casualties, but much of their equipment had been swept away. Only six paths had been blown in that barricade before the tide halted their operations. Unable to break through the obstacles that blocked their beaches, craft turned toward Easy Red where the gaps had been blown. Then as successive waves ran in toward the cluttered beach-head they soon found themselves snarled in a jam offshore."

Admiral Kirk, however, had no intention of letting his colleagues on land bleed to death; he bunched together his destroyers on the coast, and they fired at the maximum rate on all the German fire-points that showed themselves. At the same time, the German 352nd Division battery positions began running out of shells, and as the Allies' cruisers and their tactical air forces attacked all the crossroads, the Germans were not able to supply their artillery with fresh ammunition. At about 1300 hours, the crisis was over and the infantrymen, after the sappers had blown up the anti-tank dike surrounding the beach, infiltrated the German position through the narrow gullies running up the cliff.

During the night of June 6–7, the remainder of the 29th Division (Major-General C. H. Gerhardt) was landed. But V Corps' losses had been heavy: 3,881 killed, wounded, and missing.

## New breaches in Atlantic Wall

The British 2nd Army (General Miles C. Dempsey) had been assigned Bayeux, Caen, and Troarn (9 miles east of Caen) as its D-Day objectives. It was also ordered to extend its reconnaissance to Villers-Bocage and Evrecy, that is along approximately 18 miles of the Calvados coast. This ambitious programme was not fulfilled.

The British 6th Airborne Division (Major-General Richard N. Gale) was to protect the flanks of the operation. It was ordered to capture intact the bridges across the Orne and its canal between Bénouville and Ranville; to destroy the Merville battery; and to destroy the Dives bridges between Troarn and the coast.

Although the wind prevented the paratroopers from landing accurately on their targets, the division completed these three missions brilliantly. At 0030 hours the British sappers and infantry had jumped from five gliders and captured the Bénouville bridges, clearing them of mines. At about 0400 hours Lieutenant-Colonel Otway had only collected 150 paratroopers from his battalion which was practically without matériel, and the gliders which were due to land on the superstructure of the defence works had failed to appear. Nevertheless, he had captured the Merville battery in a fierce fight in which he lost 70 dead and wounded, whilst the garrison of 130 men was left with only 22 survivors. The Dives mission was also completely successful.

At dawn, Rear-Admiral Vian's naval forces opened fire on the German defences, and up to nightfall discharged 500 15-

inch shells, 3,500 6-inch shells, and 1,380 small calibre missiles. They made wide breaches in the Atlantic Wall. Two further circumstances favoured the British landing. First, the amphibious tanks were lowered into the water much closer to the shore than at "Omaha", and were sometimes landed directly on the beaches. Secondly, large numbers of the special vehicles designed by Major-General Sir Percy Hobart, commander of the 79th Armoured Division, were used in the first waves of the infantry attack.

In addition to the Crabs, or flail tanks, which cleared the ground of the mines obstructing their tracks and had been used since El Alamein, the British 2nd Army also brought its Crocodiles and its A.V.R.E.s into the line: the Crocodiles were flame-thrower tanks which cast a 360-foot jet of burning oil beyond the range of the enemy's rocket-launchers; these tanks had trailers filled with about 400 gallons of fuel and could sustain prolonged actions; the A.V.R.E.s were mortar tanks carrying a 9-inch mortar on a Churchill tank chassis, and intended for work against armoured strongpoints.

On the other hand, against the British I and XXX Corps (commanded respectively by Lieutenant-Generals J. T. Crocker and G. T. Bucknall) the German 716th Division (Lieutenant-General W. Richter) only had four battalions and their quality was inferior to that of the Allies.

In these conditions, the 50th Division (Major-General D. A. H. Graham), the advance-guard of XXX Corps, proceeded from "Gold" Beach without much difficulty. By the end of the day it had some armour at the approaches of Bayeux and had moved forward about six miles.

In I Corps, the 3rd Canadian Division (Major-General R. F. L. Keller) had a more difficult landing because the Calvados reefs presented a natural obstacle; nevertheless it had advanced eight miles from Bernières ("Juno" Beach) and was near its objective, the Carpiquet airfield. On the other hand the armoured column which it had launched towards Evrecy was driven back with losses. The result was that between its left at Saint Aubin-sur-Mer and the right of the 50th Division, towards Arromanches, the Atlantic Wall had been breached over a front of 12 miles.

Landing at "Sword" Beach in the RivaBella area, the British 3rd Division (Major-General G. T. Rennie) had managed to join with the 6th Airborne Division over the Bénouville bridge. In the evening it had advanced to Biéville and repelled a counter-attack from 21st Panzers. With its right close up against Lion-sur-Mer it was four or five miles from the Canadian 3rd Division.

## D-Day casualties

The British 2nd Army had a total of less than 3,000 killed, wounded, and missing on D-Day.

Allied naval and air losses were insignificant: 114 planes, mainly brought down by A.A. fire; some landing craft and two destroyers-one of these, the Corry (U.S. Navy) blew up on a mine in the "Utah" Beach waters; the other, the Norwegian Svenner, succumbed to an attack on the Eastern Naval Task Force by three German destroyers from Le Havre commanded by Lieutenant-Commander Hoffmann.

## Hitler holds back reinforcements

At 0111 hours (German time) General Erich Marcks, commander of LXXXIV Corps, was at his H.Q. in Saint L6 cwhen he heard from the 716th Division that the paratroopers were coming down between the Orne and the Dives and that the bridges of these two rivers were apparently their objectives. Twenty minutes later the 709th Division signalled the landing of American paratroopers on both sides of the Merderet in the Sainte Mère-Eglise area. Quite correctly, Marcks decided that this was the invasion. He therefore alerted the troops on the coast and informed the 7th Army H.Q. at Le Mans.

The 7th Army quickly transmitted the information to la Roche-Guyon and Saint Germain. Although he hesitated when he received LXXXIV Corps' appreciation, supported by the 7th Army, Rundstedt alerted the Panzer-"Lehr" Division and the 12th "Hitlerjugend" Panzer Division and contacted O.K.W., but Hitler forbade him to move them till further orders, which would be given him as soon as the situation was clear.

Therefore it was only at 1432 that Army Group "B" received the authority, which it had sought for 12 hours, to order the 12th S.S. Panzer Division to support the 7th Army, and at 1507 hours to move the Waffen-S.S. I Panzer Corps and the Panzer-"Lehr" Division.

But after so much delay, Colonel-General Dollmann now showed excessive haste. Lieutenant-General Bayerlein, commander of the Panzer-"Lehr" Division, after leaving his unit to obtain instructions from 7th Army H.Q., was ordered to move towards Caen at 1700 hours. Without success the former chief-of-staff of the Afrika Korps attempted to persuade Dollmann how foolish it was to set out on the French roads before nightfall. Nevertheless Dollmann kept to his decision, thinking he would. thus be able to bring the Panzer "Lehr" Division into action south of Caen on the following day, June 7. But the first bombs began falling before Bayerlein and his staff had passed Beaumont-sur-Sarthe.

In the Saint Pierre-sur-Dives region, the 21st Panzer Division (Major-General Feuchtinger) was in a rather different situation: it was Army Group "B" 's reserve, but its commander was authorised to put his infantry into action to support the 716th Division if there was a landing; however, he was not allowed to engage his armour. In accordance with these orders Feuchtinger launched one of his grenadier regiments on the right bank of the Orne to engage the British paratroopers and as he received no orders from la Roche-Guyon, he sent his armoured regiment to follow them. At 0700 hours, he was informed that he was subordinate to the 7th Army; two hours later that he would now take his orders from LXXXIV Corps.

But now General Marcks was becoming more aware of the danger from the sea; for this reason, at 1000 hours, he ordered his new subordinate to abandon the action his armoured regiment was about to take against the enemy paratroopers, and to send it over the Orne to give support to the 716th Division units barring the approach to Caen from the British. This move was completed at 1430 hours and the Germans counter-attacked at 1700 hours. At nightfall the 21st Panzer Division had managed to reach Luc-sur-Mer with its infantry, but its armoured regiment had been engaged by the British 3rd Division and had suffered heavy losses.

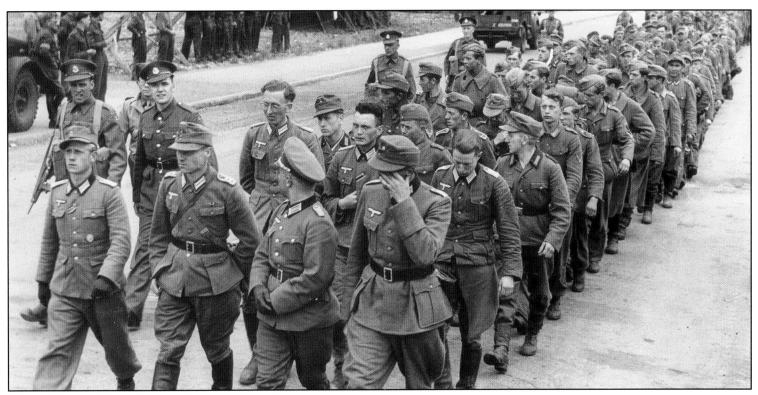

*Hundreds of German prisoners arriving from the beachhed.*

Moreover it had nearly run out of petrol. Therefore Feuchtinger, who had 146 tanks and 51 assault guns when the engagement commenced, retreated on orders, abandoning the wrecks of 40 tracked vehicles.

## The German position

At 1300 hours, a report from LXXXIV Corps to the 7th Army gave an accurate description of the fluctuations of this merciless struggle: "in the Caen area, in the British sector, the enemy is successful. East of the American sector, the landing is more or less repulsed at Vierville. Our counter-attack is in progress in the Sainte Mère-Eglise district; the 8th Regiment of the American 4th

Division (Colonel van Fleet) is pinned down there. Where is our air support? Enemy aircraft prevent us from moving or supplying our troops by day."

At midnight, an entry in the 7th Army's signals diary showed the worsening situation in the afternoon in the Caen sector:

"2400 hours. 716 Infantry Division is still defending itself at strongpoints. Communications between division, regimental and battalion headquarters, however, no longer exist, so that nothing is known as to the number of strong-points still holding out or of those liquidated … The Chief-of-Staff of Seventh Army gives the order that the counter attack of June 7 must reach the coast without fail, since the strong-point defenders expect it of us."

*Sherman Flail tank.*

The Battle of Normandy started very unpromisingly for the Wehrmacht. Nevertheless the Allies took a little more than six weeks to break out of the Avranches bottleneck, although according to plans they should have done so on D 1–20, June 27; they required another three weeks to complete the defeat of Army Group "B". This delay was due to two different factors:

1. The Normandy bocage (mixed woodland and pastureland), where the defenders were undoubtedly favoured by their natural surroundings. General Bradley wrote: "Not even in Tunisia had we found more exasperating defensive terrain. Collins called it no less formidable than the jungles of Guadalcanal."

2. The inferior quality of their armour compared with the Germans'. General Bradley is recognised as one of the best brains in the American army. "Originally", he wrote, "the Sherman had come equipped with a 75-mm gun, an almost totally ineffective weapon against the heavy frontal plate of these German tanks. Only by swarming around the panzers to hit them on the flank, could our Shermans knock the enemy out. But too often the American tankers complained it cost them a tank or two, with crews, to get the enemy's panzers but only by expending more tanks than we cared to lose. Ordnance thereafter replaced the antedated 75 with a new 76-mm high-velocity gun. But even this new weapon often scuffed rather than penetrated the enemy's armour. "Eisenhower was angry when he heard of these limitations of the new 76." The British got their best results when they re-armed their Shermans with the 17-pounder anti-tank guns which they had had since 1943. Even worse, the British and the Americans found that their Shermans were inclined to catch fire suddenly like bowls of flaming punch.

However, the Panzers' undeniable technical superiority was of little help to Rommel, as he was unable to supply them with the required fuel or to defend them against the attacks of the Allied tactical air force, of which they were rightly a priority target.

The word Jabo (Jagdbomber: fighter-bomber) recurs in all the accounts left by the German combatants after the Normandy battle. In their attacks against enemy armour, the Allies preferred rockets, which were more accurate than bombs and more effective than the 20-mm or 40-mm shell. §wker Typhoon fighter carried eight 60-pounder rockets, whilst the Republic P-47 Thunderbolt had ten 5-inch anti-tank rockets.

In this ground-air battle, the rôle of the Allied engineers has perhaps not been sufficiently appreciated. They quickly cleared the rubble left in the Normandy towns and villages by the bombardments and restored communications as the troops moved forward. They also had better equipment, notably in machines of American manufacture, and in the Bailey bridge, which had prefabricated components and could be assembled in a great variety of combinations. By May 8 1945, 7,500 Bailey bridges had been built in the Western and Italian war theatres; they certainly contributed not only to the defeat of the Third Reich, but also to the reconstruction of this part of the continent.

On June 7 and 8 successively the 12th "Hitlerjugend" S.S. Panzer Division and the Panzer-"Lehr" Division failed to drive the British back to the Channel. On June 7 the first of these major units (which under Major-General Witt included 177 tanks and 28 assault guns) should have counter-attacked in the direction of the Douvres operational base (six miles north of Caen) with the 21st Panzer Division, which was immediately to its left. It managed to maul a Canadian armoured brigade in the Carpiquet region but when it reached its goal it was halted by massive artillery fire and turned to the left.

The following day the Panzer-"Lehr" Division came into the line on the left of the 12th S.S. Panzer Division, but between Sées and Tilly-sur-Seulles it had lost five tanks, 84 all-purpose transport vehicles, 90 cars and lorries, and 40 petrol tankers; these considerable losses caused no less concern to Lieutenant-General Bayerlein than the 12th S.S. Panzer Division's had to his colleague Witt. Moreover Vice Admiral Ruge noted in his personal diary at the la Roche-Guyon H.Q., to which Rommel had returned late in the afternoon on June 6: "The enemy's air superiority is having the effect the Field-Marshal had foreseen: our movements are extremely slow, supplies don't get through, any deployment is becoming impossible, the artillery can't move to its firing positions any more. Precisely the same thing is happening on land here as happened at sea in the Tunisian campaign."

On June 8, when the U.S. 1st Army and the British 2nd Army joined up at Bayeux, Rundstedt put Rommel in charge of Panzergruppe "West", which became responsible for the conduct of operations in the sector between the mouth of the Dives and the Tilly-sur-Seulles area, while the 7th Army from now on faced the Americans alone. General Geyr von Schweppenburg, when he assumed this heavy task, was assigned the mission of retaking Bayeux and he proposed that he should break through to the Channel with his three Panzer divisions. But as soon as he set up his headquarters in the Thury-Harcourt region, he was seriously wounded in an air attack which killed many of his staff. Sepp Dietrich took over and ordered his troops to stay on the defensive while they waited for better opportunities to attack.

## Intervention of the heavy Panzers

In fact on June 12, with the intervention of the 2nd Panzer Division (Lieutenant-General von Lüttwitz) which had been brought up from the Amiens region, Dietrich managed to halt an assault by the British XXX Corps which had launched the 7th Armoured Division (Major-General G. W. Erskine) against its left wing and its rear. The celebrated Desert Rats got the worst of this chance encounter, which was fought for Villers-Bocage, not for lack of energy and courage but because they were let down by their matériel. CThe British 2nd Army's defeat was fully compensated for on the same day by the fall of Carentan, whose defenders succumbed to the concentric thrust of the American 29th Division and 101st Airborne Division. The 17th S.S. Panzergrenadier Division "Götz von Berlichingen" (Lieutenant-General Ostermann) was alerted on June 7 at its stations at Thouars but arrived too late to prevent General Bradley's V and VII Corps from joining up. When it crossed the Loire it received the same treatment from the fighter-bombers as the Panzer-"Lehr" Division. The Anglo-Americans now had a continuous front between the Dives and Saint Marcouf.

## Allied reinforcements

During the first days of battle the Germans had already

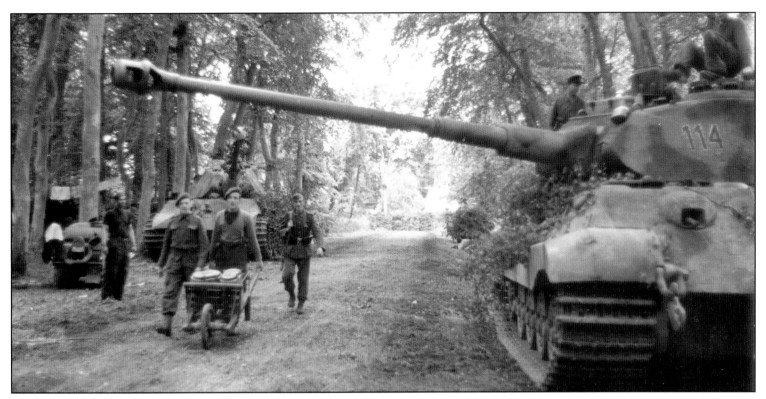

*Panzer Mk VIb King Tiger tanks hide from allied aircraft.*

lost 10,000 prisoners and 150 tanks. Even more important, Montgomery and Eisenhower were as aware as Rommel and Rundstedt that, contrary to expectations, the defenders were not getting reinforcements as quickly as the attackers at this stage.

From June 7 to 12 the British and Americans put in their floating reserves, which had sailed on the same day as the first echelon; these consisted of five infantry and three airborne divisions. The American V Corps was joined by the 9th and 20th Divisions; the British XXX Corps by the 7th Armoured and the 49th Divisions; and the British I Corps by the 51st Highland Division, giving 15 divisions (eight American) out of a total of 37 stationed in the U.K.: 362,547 men, 54,186 vehicles, and about 102,000 tons of supplies landed in a week.

According to S.H.A.E.F.'s estimates, Montgomery was faced by 21 divisions on June 12. In fact, the defence was reinforced on June 6 by 21st Panzer Division; June 7 by 12th Panzer Division; June 8 by Panzer-"Lehr" Division; June 9 by 353rd Panzer Division; June 11 by 17th S.S. Panzergrenadier Division; June 12 by 2nd Panzer and 3rd Parachute Divisions

Including the five divisions guarding the area between Cabourg and Mont Saint Michel on D-Day, Panzergruppe "West" and the German 7th Army had 12 divisions (including five armoured divisions) in the line; however, the 716th Division was only a cypher and the 352nd and 709th Divisions had been badly mauled. The Panzers went into the attack at random, always behind schedule, and under strength.

## German communications disorganised

The air offensive against the French and Belgian railway networks broadly paid the dividends expected of it. This action continued, but from the night of June 5–6 it was made doubly successful by the intervention of the Resistance against the German communications in accordance with the "Green Plan" compiled by French Railways, while the "Tortoise Plan" drawn up by the French Post Office was carried out just as successfully against the occupying forces' telephone communications.

Pierre de Préval has listed 278 acts of sabotage carried out by the French Resistance from June 6 to September 15, 1944 in the department of Meurthe-et-Moselle, and the position was similar in the other departments. On the route from Montauban to the Normandy front, the Waffen-S.S. 2nd Panzer Division "Das Reich" (Lieutenant-General Lammerding) was harried by the Corrèze maquis; the terrible reprisals taken on the inhabitants of Tulle and Oradour by this division to avenge these ambushes remain unforgotten.

From now on the delay in building up the German defence on the invasion front is perfectly understandable, as the combined action of the Anglo-American forces and the French Resistance networks was effectively assisted by Hitler's personal interference in war operations.

## Hitler's error

We have mentioned that when he was expecting the landing, the Führer had an intuition that Normandy might well be the invasion's objective. But he revised his view as soon as Eisenhower had launched Operation "Overlord". Plainly, he thought, he was faced with a diversionary manoeuvre aimed at making him lower his guard in the Pas-de-Calais.

Nevertheless on June 8 Major Hayn, LXXXIV Corps' chief Intelligence officer, was brought a copy of U.S. VII Corps' battle orders which had been discovered on board a barge that had grounded near Isigny after its crew had been killed. This document, not only revealed General Collins's intentions, but also listed V Corps' and the British XXX Corps' objectives. The Americans' mission was to reach the Cotentin western coast as soon as possible, and then to change direction to the north and capture Cherbourg. Without delay this battle order was passed through the correct channels; 7th Army, Army Group "B", Supreme Command West, and O.K.W. Hitler, however, obstinately stuck to his opinion that this was a deceptive manoeuvre, and in support of his view he quoted the Abwehr's summaries stating that just before the landing there were 60 or even 67 British and American divisions stationed in Britain. He never asked himself whether the real deception lay in simulating the existence of 30 divisions concentrated in Kent and ready to cross the English Channel at its narrowest point. At the front, on the other hand, where the Germans saw most of the Allied units they had previously met in Africa and Sicily (U.S. 1st and 9th Divisions, British 7th Armoured Division and 50th and 51st Divisions), they dismissed the idea of a second landing in the north of France. But nothing was done and Rommel was forbidden to use the 18 divisions of the 15th Army which, with the exception of the 346th and 711th Divisions, which were engaged on the right bank of the Orne, remained in reserve until after the breakthrough.

## Rommel's plan abandoned

After a week's fighting, Rommel transmitted his appreciation and his intentions to Keitel: "The Army Group is endeavouring to replace the Panzer formations by infantry formations as soon as possible, and re-form mobile reserves with them. The Army Group intends to switch its Schwerpunkt in the next few days to the area Carentan–Montebourg to annihilate the enemy there and avert the danger to Cherbourg. Only when this has been done can the enemy between the Orne and the Vire be attacked."

The following conclusions can be drawn from this telephone message:

1. Rommel stated he was compelled to give up his first plan to push the enemy back into the sea immediately. Hitler therefore was not able to recover on the Western Front the forces which he hoped to collect for the Eastern Front.

2. In order to release his armoured formations from the front, he would have had to have the same number of infantry formations at his disposal at the appropriate time. For this purpose the veto imposed on him by Hitler on taking troops from the 15th Army did not simplify matters.

3. Even if he had obtained these infantry formations, what he stated in any case shows that Montgomery's idea of free manoeuvre, which he put into practice in Normandy, was soundly

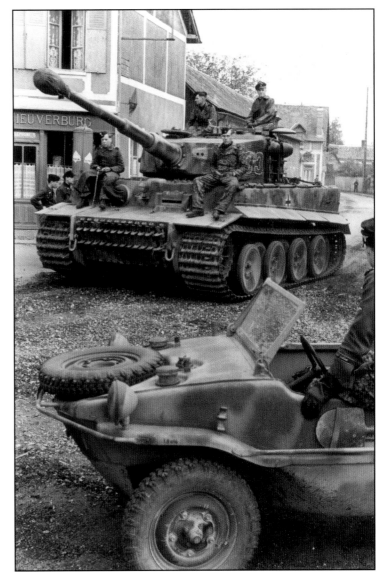

*Panzer Mk VI Tiger tank on its way to Normandy.*

and judiciously conceived.

4. Without these formations he could not displace Army Group "B"'s point of main effort from the Caen–Tilly-sur-Seulles area to the Carentan–Montebourg area, and therefore the "strong point" of Cherbourg was from now on virtually written off.

*Allied troops avoiding snipers near Caen.*

The unsavoury gossip about Bradley was nothing to the criticisms made of Montgomery regarding the mediocre victories which the British 2nd Army could claim at that time. It had in fact to attack three times, and it was not until July 9, 1944 that it was able to announce the capture of Caen, its D-Day objective. Of course, Montgomery could hardly reveal to the journalists that his plan aimed first and foremost at forcing Rommel to concentrate his Panzers against the British 2nd Army, and wearing them down on this front by a series of purely local actions. Here, for example, is part of Major-General Roberts's description of Operation "Goodwood" on July 19 and 20.

"But 3 R.T.R. were through. They had started with 52 tanks, been given 11 replacements, making 63 tanks in all. With Bras now in their hands, they had nine tanks left. Major Close's A Squadron had lost 17 tanks in two days, seven being completely destroyed, the others recoverable; all Troop officers had been killed or wounded, and only one troop Sergeant was left. The Fife and Forfar had fared rather worse."

In the circumstances it is not surprising that the famous units that had formed part of the 8th Army in North Africa (the 50th and 51st Infantry Divisions, and the 7th Armoured Division) did not have the success expected of them in this new theatre of operations. Writing of these veterans of Bir Hakeim, Tobruk, and El Alamein, Belfield and Essame remind us of the old saying current in the British Army — "An old soldier is a cautious soldier, that is why he is an old soldier." Quite probably. But perhaps the hiding the Desert Rats received at Villers-Bocage on June 12, when they first came into contact with the 2nd Panzer Division, was such as to make even the most reckless prudent.

It is also possible to criticise the British High Command for the tendency in its instructions to try to foresee everything, even the unforeseeable. Having seen orders issued by the main American commanders, we know that they subscribed to the same theory as the Germans, that the order should contain all that the lesser commander needs to know to carry out his task but nothing more; whereas British orders tended to go into further detail, limiting the initiative of the tactical commanders, because of theoretical situations that did not always arise. For in war, it is said, it is the unexpected that happens.

In this list of Montgomery's resources, an honourable mention must be made of the artillery, for which Rommel's grenadiers had a special dislike, for it fired quickly and accurately. In particular, the 25-pounder "gun-howitzer" fired so rapidly that the Germans thought it must have been fitted with a system of automatic loading. And this fact goes a long way to explain the form which the fighting took in the Caen sector, for if the British tanks failed in all their attempts at breakthrough whenever they came up against the German Panthers, Tigers, and the 8.8-cm anti-tank guns of Panzergruppe "West", the German counter-attacks collapsed under the murderous fire of the British artillery concentrations whenever they went beyond purely local engagements. All the more so since at that distance from the coast the big guns of the Royal Navy were able to take a hand. So it was that on June 16 in the region of Thury-Harcourt, about 20 miles from Riva-Bella, a 16-inch shell from the Rodney or the Nelson killed Lieutenant-General Witt, commanding the 12th S.S. Panzer

Division "Hitlerjugend".

The failure of British XXX Armoured Corps and the 7th Armoured Division to turn the front of Panzergruppe "West" at Villers-Bocage seems to have caused Montgomery to shift the centre of gravity of his attack to the countryside around Caen, where his armour would find a more suitable terrain.

Operation "Epsom", begun on June 25, brought into action VIII Corps, just landed in Normandy and commanded by Sir Richard O'Connor, released from captivity by the signing of the Italian armistice. Covered on his right by XXX Corps' 49th Division, O'Connor was to cross the Caen–Bayeux road to the west of the Carpiquet aerodrome, push on past the Fossé de l'Odon, then switching the direction of his attack from south to south-west, he would finally reach Bretteville-sur-Laize, ten miles south of Caen, near the Caen–Falaise road. This would give the British 2nd Army, not only the capital of Normandy, but also the Carpiquet air base, upon which Air-Marshals Coningham and Leigh-Mallory had long been casting envious eyes.

VIII Corps had 60,000 men, 600 tanks, and 700 guns. The 15th and 43rd Divisions, each reinforced by a brigade of Churchill tanks, provided O'Connor with his shock troops, whilst the 11th Armoured Division would then exploit the situation. For all three divisions it was their first taste of combat.

Whilst the left wing of XXX Corps attacked the Panzer-"Lehr" Division, VIII Corps' attack brought it into contact with the 12th S.S. Panzer Division "Hitlerjugend", commanded, since the death of General Witt, by General Kurt Meyer, a leader of extreme resolution, of rapid and correct decisions, whom his men

had nicknamed "Panzer-Meyer". By nightfall, at the price of fierce combat and despite incessant counter-attacks, the British infantry was able to bed down near the Caen-Villers-Bocage road, three miles from their starting point. On June 27, the 15th Division managed to capture a sound bridge over the Odon, and the 11th Armoured Division advanced and began the switching movement mentioned earlier: the first objective was Hill 112, the summit of the ridge which separates the Odon and Orne Valleys.

## German counter-attack fails

The VIII Corps, however, was now behind schedule, and some very troublesome bottlenecks were building up at its rear. These difficulties enabled Sepp Dietrich, commanding I S.S. Panzer Corps, to avoid the worst by bringing in General Paul Hausser's II S.S. Panzer Corps, which had just come back from the Galician front. He even tried to take the 11th Armoured Division in a pincer movement between the 9th S.S. Panzer Division "Hohenstaufen" and the 10th S.S. Panzer Division "Frundsberg" and only failed because O'Connor evacuated his troops from a salient that had become too exposed.

On the other hand the Panzergruppe "West" failed in its efforts to turn this defensive success into a general offensive, for II S.S. Panzer Corps was literally pinned down by artillery fire and tactical air bombardment whenever it made the slightest move. In this connection General Harzer, Chief Operations Staff Officer of the 9th S.S. Panzergrenadier Division said later: "Now, if the Luftwaffe had been able to deal with the Allied navies and also stop the accurate bombing of certain targets, I think that the

British-Canadian landings would once again have 'fallen in the ditch', as they say. As it was, our counter-offensive broke down under air attack and artillery fire, particularly the heavy guns of the battleships. They were devastating. When one of these shells dropped near a Panther, the 56-ton (sic) tank was blown over on its side, just from the blast. It was these broadsides from the warships, more than the defensive fighting of the enemy's troops, which halted our division's Panzer Regiment." At all events, after this sharp lesson, the Germans gave up any further idea of throwing the enemy back into the sea. Instead, they had been forced to feed into a defensive battle the reserves they needed for a major counter-strike.

Montgomery, in his June 30 directive to Generals Bradley and Dempsey, declared himself to be quite satisfied with the results obtained, although Operation "Epsom" had only dented the enemy line.

"All this is good … by forcing the enemy to place the bulk of his strength in front of the Second Army, we have made easier the acquisition of territory on the western flank.

"To hold the maximum number of enemy divisions on our eastern flank between Caen and Villers Bocage, and to swing the western or right flank of the Army Group southwards and eastwards in a wide sweep so as to threaten the line of withdrawal of such enemy divisions to the south of Paris."

The carrying out of this plan meant continuing to place the main weight of this battle of attrition on the shoulders of General Dempsey, for the slightest slackening of pressure would mean that Rommel would be able to reorganise and re-form.

## The British attack again

Because of a delay by the U.S. 1st Army out on the Allied right flank, in preparing Operation "Cobra", the attack which was to crush German resistance, Montgomery asked Dempsey for one more effort to engage and tie down the Panzers on his front, and, if possible, to advance the armoured units of his 2nd Army into the region around Falaise. To this end, Operation "Goodwood" had moved the centre of gravity of the attack back to the right bank of the Orne, where the British 1st and 8th Armies were massed, whilst the Canadian II Corps, two divisions strong, was concentrated within the ruins of Caen. To it fell the task of capturing the suburbs of the town to the south of the river, and of developing an attack towards Falaise. The enemy's front, tied down in the centre, would be by-passed and rolled back from left to right by the three armoured divisions (the 7th and 11th, and the Guards Armoured Divisions), breaking out from the narrow bridgehead between the Orne and the Dives, which General Gale's parachute troops had captured on the night of June 5–6. VIII Corps possessed 1,100 tanks, 720 guns and a stockpile of 250,000 shells. But above all, the Allied air forces would support and prepare the attack on a scale hitherto undreamed of: 1,600 four-engined planes, and 600 two-engined planes and fighter-bombers would drop more than 7,000 tons of explosives on enemy positions, and then support VIII Corps' armour as it advanced.

However, the Germans had seen through the Allies' intentions, and had organised themselves to a depth of ten miles; it is true that they only had in the line one division, the 16th Luftwaffe

Field Division, and what was left of the 21st Panzer Division, but they still possessed considerable fire-power, in the shape of 272 6-tube rocket launchers and a hundred or so 8.8-cm anti-aircraft guns operating as anti-tank guns. So the Allies were to find difficulty in making their overall superiority tell.

On July 18, at 0530 hours, the thunder of 720 guns signalled the beginning of Operation "Goodwood". Then, as one member of VIII Corps put it, the aircraft "came lounging across the sky, scattered, leisurely, indifferent. The first ones crossed our lines, and the earth began to shake to a continuous rumble which lasted for three-quarters of an hour; and at no time during that period were fewer than fifty 'planes visible. The din was tremendous. We could see the bombs leaving the 'planes and drifting down almost gently, like milt from a salmon, and as they disappeared behind the trees the rumble rose a little and then sunk to its old level again. The Jocks were all standing grinning at the sky. After weeks of skulking in trenches, here was action; action on a bigger scale than any of them had dreamed was possible."

At 0745 hours the 11th Armoured Division, preceded by a continuous barrage of an intensity never before experienced, began to advance, and quickly got through the first position, defended by troops still groggy from the pounding inflicted by Bomber Command. But towards mid-day the attack came up against the railway line running from Caen to Paris, where it stopped.

## Meagre success for the British

This was due, first, to the fact that the British artillery, which had stayed on the left bank of the Orne, no longer had the enemy within range; and second, that on the bridges which the Guards and the 7th Armoured Division had to take to get across to the right bank and link up with the 11th Division, there were tremendous bottlenecks. Above all, however, was the fact that 8.8-cm guns and Nebelwerfers were firing from the many villages on the outskirts of the town. At nightfall the 1st S.S. Panzer Division "Leibstandarte", which formed Sepp Dietrich's reserve, surprised the 11th Armoured Division, just when it was about to bed down, and according to its commander, Major-General Wisch, destroyed about 40 tanks.

On July 19, with the rain taking a hand, the terrain got into such a state owing to the bombing the day before, that operations had to stop. South and south-west of Caen, the British and Canadians had advanced about five miles into the enemy's defensive positions, but had not succeeded in overrunning them. All in all it was rather a meagre success, especially as it had been paid for at the enormous price of 413 tanks, but there was a certain strategic compensation, as the 116th Panzer Division of the German 15th Army, stationed up till then near Amiens, was ordered to move towards Caen; and then Kluge, Rundstedt's successor at the head of Army Group "B", afraid of a British breakthrough in the direction of Falaise, thought it advisable to move his 2nd Panzer Division from Saint Lô to Caen, less than a week before the beginning of Operation "Cobra".

By this same day of July 19, the losses of the British 2nd Army Between June 6 and July 25, German strength had shifted away from the American front. The moment for the final break-through was approaching.

*Ammunition truck hit by enemy mortar fire.*

On July 25 General Bradley began Operation "Cobra". On that day the German forces defending Normandy consisted of: from the coastal battery at Merville to the area of Caumont-l'Eventé: 5th Panzerarmee (General Eberbach) comprising LXXXVI Corps, I and II Waffen-S.S. Panzer Corps, LXXIV Corps, with between them 11 divisions, including two Panzer and two Panzergrenadier, with about 645 tanks (these faced the British and Canadian forces); and from Caumont-l'Eventé to the western coast of the Cotentin peninsula: 7th Army (General Hausser) astride the Vire with three corps of 13 divisions: on the right bank of the river XLVII Panzer Corps and II Parachute Corps with between them six infantry divisions and on the left bank LXXXIV Corps with one Panzergrenadier and two Panzer divisions with about 190 tanks.

But there are divisions and divisions. Let us take the case of LXXXIV Corps, which was going to bear the brunt of the attack. Its 91st, 243rd, and 352nd Divisions had only 2,500 rifles between them, after the fierce fighting in the bocage, and its three armoured divisions ("Lehr" and 2nd S.S. "Das Reich" Panzer, and 17th S.S. "Götz von Berlichingen" Panzergrenadier) were down to something like half their establishment. The German front twisted and turned along the stretch Bradley was to attack, and the German 7th Army was very weak because Montgomery had drawn the weight of the German forces into the Caen sector. Bradley brought up no less than 12 divisions, including four armoured.

The attack of July 25 had the benefit of exceptionally powerful air preparation, the details of which were drawn up by General Bradley and Air Chief Marshal Leigh-Mallory. On July 24 4,000 tons of bombs fell on LXXXIV Corps' positions. During the morning of the following day no fewer than 1,880 four-engined and twin-engined bombers, and 550 fighter-bombers dropped 4,150 tons of bombs opposite the American VII Corps front to a depth of a mile and a half and on the bridges upstream of the Vire from Saint L6. By special orders from Bradley, who did not want the terrain to be pitted with deep craters, only light bombs and napalm were used.

"Nothing could withstand it," wrote the German historian Paul Carell. "Trenches, gun-emplacements: ploughed up. Petrol-, ammunition- and supply-dumps: set on fire." The Panzer-"Lehr" Division, in particular, down to 5,000 men, was heavily knocked about: "at least half its personnel was put out of action: killed, wounded, buried alive or driven out of their minds. All the tanks and guns in the forward positions were wiped out. Every road in the area was made useless."

Neither Colonel-General Hausser nor Field-Marshal von Kluge expected an attack of such violence from the American 1st Army between the Vire and the Channel. General von Choltitz, commanding LXXXIV Corps, who had seen it coming and whose warning had not been heeded by his superiors, now had to rely on his own resources to plug the gap created by the annihilation of the Panzer-"Lehr" Division. On July 26 Collins was able to pass his 2nd and 3rd Armoured Divisions (respectively Major Generals Edward H. Brooks and Leroy H. Watson) through his infantry lines. By evening the 3rd had passed through Marigny and was on its way to Coutances and the 2nd was patrolling through Saint

*Ammunition stocks of STUG IV being replenished.*

Gilles and Canisy, some seven to eight miles from its point of departure.

The 2nd and 116th Panzer Divisions were hastily withdrawn from the 5th Panzerarmee in the Caen area but did not get to the breach until July 29, by which time it was widening every hour. There was therefore no alternative for LXXXIV Corps but to retreat, and do so quickly, as its left flank had been pierced in the area of Périers by the American VIII Corps. The direction this retreat was to take gave rise to a conflict between the LXXXIV Corps and 7th Army commanders. The latter, anxious to retain some coherence in his dispositions, wanted Choltitz to withdraw south-eastwards, whereupon the latter protested vehemently that if he were to do this he would be opening the way for the enemy to get into Brittany. This is what happened, in fact; Kluge wrongly attributed the blame to Choltitz and replaced him by Lieutenant-General Elfeldt. Choltitz had no difficulty in clearing himself and was rewarded with the command of Gross Paris.

## Coutances and Avranches captured

On July 28 the U.S. 4th Armoured Division (Major-General John S. Wood) took Coutances and that same night got across the Sienne at Cérences. Twenty-four hours later 6th Armoured Division (Major-General Robert W. Grow), moving on the right flank of the 4th, crossed the See and took Avranches. On July 31 Lieutenant-General Speidel telephoned Kluge: "The left flank has collapsed."

A few minutes later the C.-in-C. West was again called: this time by General Farmbacher, commanding XXV Corps, to say

that, responsible now for organising the defence of Brittany, he found that the Kriegsmarine and the Luftwaffe, sheltering respectively behind Dönitz and Göring, were being removed from his authority. At 1045 hours the wretched Field-Marshal got in touch with O.K.W. and gave General Warlimont, Chief of Operations, a realistic picture of the situation, demanding reinforcements, and urgently, reminding O.K.W. of the example of the taxis of the Marne.

Faced with the development of Operation "Cobra", Hitler at O.K.W. finally gave up the obsession with a second landing north of the Somme which had dominated all his strategy since dawn on June 6 and responded to Kluge's call for help,

## Patton's new objectives

Hitler's decisions, however, came too late. On July 31, General Patton, who now controlled VIII Corps (and was soon to become commander of a new Third Army) was given the welcome information from the corps H.Q. that the 4th Armoured Division had reached its objective at Sélune and that the bridge at Pontaubault was still in good order. He made up his mind at once "All through military history", he cried, "wars have been lost because rivers weren't crossed." He sent off the 6th Armoured and 79th Infantry Divisions (Major-General Ira T. Wyche) towards Brest and the 4th Armoured and 8th Infantry (Major-General Donald Stroh) towards Rennes. The breach was complete, the German 7th Army was beaten and LXXXIV Corps, from which most of the 20,000 prisoners taken by the Americans since July 25 had come, was virtually wiped out. On August 1 General Bradley, now commanding 21 divisions, including six armoured, took over the American 12th Army Group in accordance with decisions taken in London on the eve of "Overlord". He handed over his 1st Army to General Courtney H. Hodges. The 1st Army at this time included V, VII, and XIX Corps. It had transferred VIII Corps to the 3rd Army, fighting alongside it, and Bradley had also moved over to 3rd Army XII, XV, and XX Corps (respectively Major-Generals R. Cook, Wade H. Haislip, and Walton H. Walker). The new C.-in-C. 12th Army Group, promoted over the head of the impetuous Patton, six years his senior, did not much relish the idea of having to send him directives but acknowledged that "George" was a great-hearted and highly intelligent soldier who, in spite of his celebrated outbursts of temper, served him with "unbounded loyalty and eagerness".

The same occasion brought the formation of the British 21st Army Group, under General Montgomery, with the British 2nd Army, still under Sir Miles Dempsey, and the Canadian 1st Army (Lieutenant-General H. D. G. Crerar). On August 15, 21st Army Group was to have five corps of 16 divisions, including six armoured, and several brigades.

## Hitler envisages withdrawal

In the afternoon of July 31 Colonel-General Jodl, having informed Hitler of his concern at the capture of Avranches, noted in his diary: "The Führer reacted favourably to the idea of an order for eventual withdrawal in France. This confirms that he thinks such an order is necessary at the present time."

The matter of withdrawal seemed virtually settled and

Lieutenant-General Warlimont was designated as liaison officer with C.-in-C. West. But on the following morning, when the O.K.W. delegate was leaving, the Führer said: "Tell Field-Marshal von Kluge that his job is to look forwards, not backwards!"

On August 3, the expected order from O.K.W. reached Kluge in the morning, but instead of confirming the withdrawal intimated by Jodl, it ordered a counter-attack. The plan was to assemble an armoured mass on the left flank of the 7th Army under General von Funck, C.-in-C. XLVII Panzer Corps, attack towards Avranches through Mortain, and cut the communications of the American 3rd Army.

Kluge was dumbfounded when he read Hitler's directive but was in no position to claim freedom of action in face of this order, as stupid as it was absolute. He was aware that Hitler knew of the part he had played in the July 20 bomb plot and that the slightest disobedience would cost him his life. The discussion therefore centred less on the principles involved than on the date of the operation, which was to be called "Lüttich" (Liège). Hitler wanted to hold back until as many American divisions as possible had been drawn into the net; Kluge urged the threat to the left flank and even to the rear of the 7th Army and asked for a start on August 7, to which Hitler agreed.

## Allied aircraft beat the Panzers

At dawn on D-day, helped by fog, XLVII Corps (116th and 2nd Panzer Divisions, 1st "Leibstandarte" and 2nd "Das Reich" S.S. Panzer Divisions) attacked between the See and the Sélune towards Avranches. Mortain fell fairly easily. But neither the

*Waffen SS advancing during Normandy invasion.*

American 30th Division (Major-General Leland S. Hobbs), though it had one battalion surrounded, nor the American VII Corps (Major-General J. L. Collins) were thrown off their stride, and towards mid-day "Das Reich" was stopped less than two miles from Saint Hilaire-du-Harcouët, over 14 miles from its objective of Pontaubault.

The fog had lifted by now, and the Panzers were caught by British Typhoon fighter-bombers, whose armour-piercing rockets again proved their deadly efficiency. The previous day General Billowius thought he could guarantee the C.-in-C. 7th Army that 300 Luftwaffe fighters would be continuously sweeping the skies above the battlefield. These had been intercepted by Anglo-American fighters as soon as they took off from the Paris area.

Faced with this lack of success, Kluge gave it as his opinion that the German forces should hold on to what they had got, or even let go. The answer was an order to throw in II S.S. Panzer Corps (General Bittrich: 9th "Hohenstaufen" and 10th "Frundsberg" Panzer Divisions), to be withdrawn from the already depleted 5th Panzerarmee. Once more C.-in-C. West had to give in, in spite of vehement protests from General Eberbach, who was expecting a strong Anglo-Canadian attack southwards along the Caen-Falaise axis.

## Patton sweeps on through the breach

Patton had the chance to streak out through the enormous gap (65 miles) between Rennes and Nantes, which he did with XV Corps on the left, XX Corps in the centre, and XII Corps on the right with its right flank along the Loire. By August 7, XV Corps was in Laval and Château-Gontier whilst XII Corps liberated Nantes and Angers, ignoring enemy resistance in Saint Nazaire.

Thus Operation "Lüttich "did not deflect Montgomery and Bradley from their initial plan. On D-day the German XLVII Corps lost some 50 tanks out of the 120 with which it had started out at dawn. The American VII Corps, strengthened to five divisions, including one armoured, immediately went over to the counterattack. This was the last chance for Army Group "B" to break out of the ring now beginning to take shape as Patton pushed ahead towards Le Mans. But Hitler obstinately refused to consider any withdrawal.

*Troops of a field artillery battery emplace 155mm howitzer.*

Operation "Totalize" which was to capture Falaise, began at 2330 hours on 7 August. The Canadian 1st Army attacked south of Caen with its 11 Corps of four divisions, including two armoured. Montgomery now had a chance to start a pincer movement which was to bring about the defeat of Army Group "B" between the Orne and the Dives on August 18 and the disgrace and suicide of the wretched Kluge.

At zero hour four mechanised columns, consisting of one armoured brigade on each flank and two motorised infantry brigades in the centre, crossed the first German line. When they had covered between two and three miles in the dark, the Canadian and Scottish infantry, from the 2nd Canadian and 51st (Highland) Divisions, left their vehicles to attack the strongpoints of the German line, illuminated for them by green tracer shells. At dawn it was clear that the H.Q. of I S.S. Panzer Corps had been overrun, the 89th Division, recently arrived on the scene, had collapsed, and the 272nd looked like giving way.

Once more the famous Panzer-Meyer (Brigadier Kurt Meyer) and his 12th "Hitlerjugend" Panzer Division saved the situation with the help of 80 assault guns and the 8.8-cm guns sent to them as reinforcement. These young veterans, who had been in the line since June 8, were pitted against the Canadian 4th Armoured Division (Major-General G. Kitching) and the Polish 1st Armoured Division (Major-General S. Maczek), both of which were in action for the first time. The military cemeteries in the area bear witness to the valiant fighting of the Allied forces, but they did not succeed in breaking through and "Totalize" ground to a halt some ten miles short of Falaise on August 9.

## General Leclerc's charge

On the same day the American XV Corps, having captured Le Mans, turned north. On its left the French 2nd Armoured Division (General Leclerc) was moving down to Alençon with the 79th Division in its wake. On the right the American 5th Armoured Division (Major-General

Lundsford E. Oliver) was on the road to Argentan, followed by the 90th Division which, newly commanded by Major-General Raymond S. MacLain, was to recover from the unfortunate reputation it had acquired in the bocage. Conscious of the threat to his rear areas, Kluge attempted to ward it off by improvising a Panzergruppe "Eberbach" consisting of LXXXI Corps (General Kuntzen), 708th Division (Lieutenant-General Wilck), and 9th Panzer Division (Lieutenant-General Jolasse) brought up from the south.

The French 2nd Armoured Division, vigorously led by General Leclerc, ran into the 9th Panzer Division on August 11, just as the Germans were moving into their positions. As night fell the French took the bridges at Alençon whilst they were still intact. On their right, the American 5th Armoured Division had crossed the Sarthe and captured Sées, having overcome the feeble resistance of the German 708th Division. On the following day Leclerc had to fight it out with the 2nd "Das Reich" S.S. Panzer Division's forward units and the 116th Panzer Division, both of which Kluge had thrown into XV Corps' sector without any further regard for O.K.W.'s orders. The French nevertheless pushed their left flank as far as Carrouges and their right to the outskirts of Argentan.

At dawn on August 13 the American XV Corps was within 16 miles of Falaise, whilst the German 7th Army, caught up in the Condé-sur-Noireau-Tinchebray-Domfront area, had between 34 and 37 miles to go under enemy-controlled skies before it broke out of the pocket. In the afternoon, however, Haislip was ordered by Patton to stop and even to pull back the units "in the neighbourhood of Falaise or north of Argentan".

Why Bradley, via Patton, should have forbidden XV Corps to close the ring round Army Group "B" in the Falaise area has often been discussed. Considerable numbers of Germans succeeded in getting away. Their escape, however, meant an almost complete abandonment of their heavy equipment and was accomplished only by terrific sacrifices.

"I was in Bradley's headquarters when messages began to arrive from commanders of the advancing American columns, complaining that the limits placed upon them by their orders were allowing Germans to escape. I completely supported Bradley in his decision that it was necessary to obey the orders, prescribing the boundary between the army groups, exactly as written; otherwise a calamitous battle between friends could have resulted."

## Kluge orders retreat

From August 15, Army Group "B" was on the retreat. Kluge did not wait for O.K.W. to confirm, but went ahead, setting in motion an operation involving two armies, seven corps, and no fewer than 23 divisions of all types. On August 17 General Dietrich, who had succeeded Eberbach as C.-in-C. 5th

Panzerarmee, got I S.S. Panzer Corps out of the net and re-assembled the bits at Vimoutiers. But the Canadians took Falaise and the Polish Ist Armoured Division, advancing up the right bank of the Dives, established contact with the American V Corps (Ist Army) which at that moment formed the southern arm of the pincer which was remorselessly closing in.

## A German disaster

On August 20, according to Martin Blumenson, the author of the volume devoted to this episode in the official history of the U.S. Army, there occurred the "artillery-man's dream":

"Five battalions pulverized columns driving towards the Dives. American soldiers cheered when German horses, carts, trucks, volkswagens, tanks, vehicles, and weapons went flying into the air, disintegrating in flashes of fire and puffs of smoke."

Nevertheless I S.S. Panzer Corps, which had got out of this attack, collected together some 20,000 Germans from all units and, refusing to be dismayed, managed to find a crack in the Allied lines, through which they got 25 tanks and 60 guns. Included in these forces was General Hausser, C.-in-C. 7th Army, who was seriously wounded in the face. On the following day, however, all firing ceased in the Argentan-Nécy-Brieux-Chambois area. Here the Allies took 50,000 prisoners; there were 10,000 dead. Fifteen divisions of Army Group "B" were wiped out in the course of this pitiless battle. Most of the German matériel was lost. The French 2nd Armoured alone took 100 guns and 700 vehicles and the 90th Division 380 armoured vehicles, 700 guns, and more than 5,000 lorries.

*Remnants of Von Kluges army after an attack on D-Day.*

## Model succeeds Kluge

This was the situation which Field-Marshal Model inherited when he took over from Kluge at his H.Q. at Saint Germain-en-Laye on August 17. Two days previously a fortuitous incident had, if not provoked, at least hastened, the disgrace of Kluge. Whilst he was up at the front an aircraft bomb had demolished the radio truck which gave him permanent contact with O.K.W., and the ensuing prolonged silence caused Hitler to conclude that C.-in-C. West had finally betrayed him and gone to see Montgomery about surrender terms.

When he said goodbye to his successor, Kluge assured him that he would speak to Hitler with all the clarity which the situation demanded. But in the car taking him back to Germany he rightly persuaded himself that the dictator would give him, not an audience at O.K.W., but a criminal trial and an ignominious death. Potassium cyanide removed him from the Führer's vengeance.

## Churchill opposes a landing in Provence ...

On the same August 15 when Army Group "B" was trying to escape from the Normandy net, the landing of an Allied force in Provence compelled O.K.W. for the first time to impose on the C.-in-C. West a withdrawal of considerable strategic importance. Right up to the last minute Churchill had tried to urge his American allies to abandon this operation, which was called first

# SLAUGHTER AT FALAISE

*British troops and armour pass through the ruins of Falaise.*

"Anvil" then "Dragoon", in favour of his projected offensive towards Vienna and the Danube across the Apennines, the Giulian Alps, and the Ljubljana gap.

In a letter dated August 6 to his friend Harry Hopkins, Churchill expressed his conviction that as the ports of Brest, Lorient, Saint Nazaire, and Nantes might fall into Allied hands "at any time", there was no logistic value left in Toulon or Marseilles. On the other hand, why not take the bull by the horns? "Dragoon", he wrote, would have to be carried out against an enemy who "at the outset [would] be much stronger than we are, and where our advance runs cross-grained to the country, which abounds in most formidable rocky positions, ridges, and gullies."

"But", he noted in particular, "after taking the two fortresses of Toulon and Marseilles we have before us the lengthy advance up the Rhône valley before we even get to Lyons. None of this operation can influence Eisenhower's battle for probably ninety days after the landings."

## ... in favour of a campaign in the Balkans

On the next day he went to Portsmouth and saw Eisenhower about it, speaking his mind more openly than he had done to Hopkins, and not concealing his interest in a campaign in the Balkans, a subject which he had not broached in his letter. Eisenhower soon realised that the Prime Minister, in his opposition to "Dragoon", was putting forward reasons of strategy so as not to have to declare the political reasons which had made him take up this attitude.

## Eisenhower's reserve

As a good American soldier General Eisenhower reckoned that he should not interfere in matters which were the responsibility of the White House and the State Department. He was to react the same way over Berlin later. He makes this perfectly clear in his memoirs when he says:

"Although I never heard him say so, I felt that the Prime Minister's real concern was possibly of a political rather than a military nature. He may have thought that a post-war situation which would see the western Allies posted in great strength in the Balkans would be far more effective in producing a stable post-hostilities world than if the Russian armies should be the ones to occupy that region. I told him that if this were his reason for advocating the campaign into the Balkans he should go instantly to the President and lay the facts, as well as his own conclusions on the table. I well understood that strategy can be affected by political considerations, and if the President and the Prime Minister should decide that it was worth while to prolong the war, thereby increasing its cost in men and money, in order to secure the political objectives they deemed necessary, then I would instantly and loyally adjust my plans accordingly. But I did insist that as long as he argued the matter on military grounds alone I could not concede validity to his arguments."

And he was clearly right. The supreme commander may lay down strategic objectives, but it is the political leaders who set the aims of warfare. Moreover Churchill was too late. The drive

*Trapped German soldiers in Falaise, France.*

for Vienna may have been conceivable on June 5 so long as everything was done to annihilate Kesselring south of the line Rimini-La Spezia, but it was not now, on August 7, by which time the enemy, whose losses in retreat had not been overwhelming, was re-establishing his line along the ridges of the Apennines. At best the Allies would have been caught in late autumn on the narrow hemmed-in roads in the area of Klagenfurt or Ljubljana and have had to fight for peaks between 3,000 and 4,000 feet high. The mountainous terrain and the weather, to say nothing of enemy action, would have severely restricted all movement. As Michael Howard has explained in The Mediterranean Strategy in the Second World War: "a pursuit to Vienna through terrain where even comparatively small units could have imposed repeated delays would have been a very difficult matter indeed." Churchill's plans were hopelessly unrealistic.

*La Motte, 7th Army US.*

Operation "Dragoon", supervised by General Maitland Wilson, C.-in-C. Mediterranean, was to be the landing between Saint Raphael and le Lavandou of the American 7th Army under Lieutenant-General A. M. Patch, who the previous year had been so successful in cleaning up Guadalcanal. .

The defence of the 400 miles of coastline between Menton and Cerbère was the responsibility of the German 19th Army. On D-day it had six divisions, deployed with three on each side of the Rhône. Between June 6 and August 4 it had had to give up its 217th, 272nd, and 277th Divisions, receiving in exchange only the 198th and the remnants of the 716th, which had been thrashed at Caen.

The German naval forces in the south of France consisted of only a limited number of small units and a few U-boats. The American air forces increased their attacks on Toulon, however, and four U-boats were sunk on August 6. The Luftwaffe had only 70 fighters and 130 bombers, a total of only one-tenth of the Allied aircraft used in Operation "Dragoon".

## The first landings

On the single day of August 15, Allied aircraft flew 4,250 sorties and only 60 German planes managed to get off the ground. Admiral Hewitt's fleet fired 50,000 shells, including 3,000 12-inch or heavier, either during the preparations or at the request of the troops landing. The American VI Corps' attack, supported by the

"Sudre" Combat Command of the French 1st Armoured Division, was against the German 148th Division (Lieutenant-General Otto Fretter-Pico) on the right and the 242nd Division (Lieutenant-General Bdssler) on the left, the latter being responsible for the defence of Toulon. Both German units were part of LXII Corps (General Neuling) but corps H.Q. at Draguignan was cut off from its troops by the landing of the "Frederick" Division, supported by the Var maquis. The only Allied unit to run into difficulties was the U.S. 36th Division (Major-General John E. Dahlquist) in the area of Agay. Everywhere else the operation went like clockwork. By evening the Allies had landed 60,000 men, 6,000 vehicles, and 50,000 tons of matériel, all at the cost of 320 killed who, for the most part, had stumbled onto mines.

Twenty-four hours later the 7th Army beach-head extended from Anthéor on the right through Draguignan, where General Neuling and his staff were taken prisoner, to le Luc on the road to Aix and over 24 miles from Fréjus, then back to the Mediterranean between Cavalière and le Lavandou. On the beaches Patch's second echelon arrived ahead of time and landed with the 1st Moroccan (General Brosset), the 3rd Algerian (General de Monsabert), and the 9th Colonial (General Magnan) Divisions, the remainder of the French 1st Armoured Division (General Touzet du Vigier) and General Guillaume's Moroccan goumiers, North African mountain troops.

On the following day this vanguard of the French 1st Army went into battle under General de Lattre de Tassigny.

## Hitler's new directive

In view of the reports he had received, and realising that there was no longer any hope of throwing the enemy back into the sea, on August 16 Hitler ordered Colonel-General Blaskowitz to begin at once the evacuation of south and southwest France. The 242nd Division at Toulon and the 244th at Marseilles (Major-General Schaeffer) would defend the ports to the last and raze their installations to the ground.

On August 20, as a consequence of this order to Army Group "G" and the increasingly serious situation of Army Group "B", whose left flank was being rolled up by Patton and the American 3rd Army, the Führer issued a new directive. This has been summarised by Professor Percy Ernst Schramm, then editor and now publisher of the O.K.W. war diaries for 1944 and 1945:

"C.-in-C. West was ordered to hold the bridgehead west of Paris and prevent the enemy drive towards Dijon. First of all what remained of the 5th Panzerarmee and the 7th Army had to be withdrawn behind the River Touques and reorganised so that their armoured formations could be brought back into the left flank. If it turned out to be impossible to hold out in front of the Seine, the Paris bridgehead had to be held and also the line Seine–Yonne–Burgundy Canal–Dijon-Dôle–Swiss frontier. The withdrawal of the 7th Army behind the Seine was to be prepared at once. The 5th Panzerarmee would protect its crossing over to the right bank so as to prevent the enemy engaged in the Seine valley from driving north and then eastwards after crossing the river."

Downstream from Paris the 1st Army, now under Army

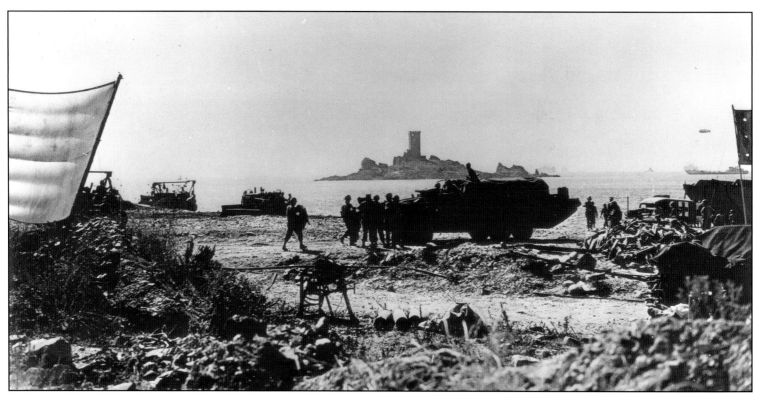

*Op Dragoon - beach activity.*

Group "B", would block off the narrow valleys on either side of Montargis to allow the occupation of the Burgundy Canal and the area north-west of Dijon.

This directive calls for two remarks. Firstly, it took no account of the 230,000 men from the army (86,337), navy and air force trapped in the "fortresses" in the West.

Amongst these, Saint Malo had fallen on August 17 after epic resistance. It took the 8-inch and 240-mm howitzers of the U.S. artillery, the 15-inch guns of the battleship Warspite, and the use of napalm to force Colonel von Aulock to hoist the white flag on the little island of Cézembre, the last centre of resistance, on September 2. The Brest garrison was attacked by the U.S. 2nd,

8th, and 29th Divisions and defended with equal tenacity by Lieutenant-General Ramcke and the 2nd Parachute Division. On September 17 fighting ceased in this unhappy town, which had been very heavily shelled. A further 48 hours were to elapse before Ramcke gave up the struggle in the Crozon peninsula.

Neither of the "fortresses" of Lorient or Saint Nazaire on opposite banks of the Loire was attacked; nor were the Channel Islands, where the 319th Division (Lieutenant-General von Schmettow) had some 30,000 men. The latter were sufficiently aware of the futility of their mission to call themselves the "Guernsey P.O.W.s" or the "non-stop card-players". But on the other hand, the shortage of usable ports was to prove a considerable handicap to the Allied supply network, and hence to the whole advance to Germany.

## German divisions bled white

Our second remark is that this directive certainly came too late. It might have been possible to carry it out on August 1, when the vanguard of the 4th Panzer Division was forcing a crossing of the Sélune at Pontaubault. But it was no longer possible on the 20th, when Patton was driving his XII and XX Corps towards Sens and Montereau and ordering XV Corps to cross the Seine at Mantes without a moment's delay.

## A new defence line

On August 24 Hitler dictated to Seyss-Inquart, the Nazi High Commissioner in Holland, Gauleiters Simon, Bürkel, and Wagner (his representatives in Luxembourg, Lorraine, and Alsace), and the military authorities concerned an order to develop a "German position in the West" for which they would have recourse to a mass levy.

There would be a continuous antitank obstacle, behind which the land would be laid waste and positions in depth organised. It would straddle the Scheldt estuary, use the line of the Albert Canal, cover Aix-la-Chapelle and Trier, the fortified complex of Thionville-Metz, turn up the Moselle as far as Saint Maurice and finally block the gap at Belfort.

Did Hitler realise that, from Model's reports, his directive of August 20 was out of date by the 24th? The fact remains that twice in four days he had recognised that he was beaten in the West.

## Paris

On August 16, the very day when the American XX Corps reached Chartres, the Paris police went on strike. This was the start of the uprising in the city. S.H.A.E.F.'s plan was not to mount a frontal attack on an urban area of this importance, but to outflank it on both sides so that it would fall of its own accord, thus sparing the city the fighting and all the destruction this would entail. According to calculations made in London, this operation was to take place between 120 and 150 days after D-Day. On August 16 at Chartres General Patton was about 20 days ahead of schedule.

General de Gaulle, in his rôle of head of the provisional government, had addressed himself to the Allied C.-in-C: "I think it is vital to occupy Paris as soon as possible with French and Allied troops, even if some fighting results and there is some damage in the city." Eisenhower agreed to the request, and Leclerc's division was sent off to Paris.

On the German side the principal actors in the drama were General Dietrich von Choltitz, the Swedish Consul-General Raoul Nordling, and the leaders of the Paris insurrection.

Hitler ordered: "The Seine bridges will be prepared for destruction. Paris must only fall into enemy hands as a heap of rubble", revealing more a state of terrorism than sound strategic thinking. As an experienced soldier Choltitz was well aware that neither the heap of rubble nor the destruction of the bridges (if they were all blown) would slow down the Allied advance. On August 23 the French 2nd Armoured Division bore down on Paris. In the night of August 24–25 Captain Dronne and the tanks Romilly, Champaubert, and Montmirail passed through the Porte de Gentilly and reached the square in front of the Hôtel de Ville. On the following day, with the aid of the Forces Françaises de l'Intérieur under Colonel Rol-Tanguy, the 2nd Armoured Division liberated Paris, and Choltitz, who had not left his headquarters in the Hôtel Meurice, surrendered.

## "Destroy Paris!"

As soon as he heard that Paris had fallen, Hitler flew into a rage and ordered it to be wiped out. With this end in view he had the great siege mortar Karl readied. This huge gun had a calibre of 60 cms (23.6 inches), fired 2.2-ton shells, and had not been in action since Sevastopol'. The V-weapons and all available aircraft were now also to be brought into action.

Speidel forbade the transmission of this order. It had not the least strategic value and it would have caused thousands of civilian victims, and the destruction of buildings of inestimable artistic value. Speidel was later arrested on suspicion of being implicated in the July Plot and was lucky to escape the horrible torture which befell Witzleben and Hoeppner. If any conclusion is to be drawn from this episode it must come in the form of a question: what stage would the intellectual and moral reconstruction of Western Europe have reached today if Generals von Choltitz and Speidel had not, at the risk of their lives, thwarted the bloodthirsty plans of Adolf Hitler?

## De Lattre presses on …

In Provence, General de Lattre de Tassigny had meanwhile managed to wriggle out of the plan by which he was intended to concentrate all his efforts on Toulon, and only move on to Marseilles when the large military port had been mopped up. De Lattre went for boldness and got the approval of General Patch, who overcame the misgivings of his staff. The French commander was, we would suggest, bolstering up a right decision with wrong premises, because on the same day, far from thinking of reinforcing the defence of Marseilles and Toulon, his adversary, acting under a directive from O.K.W., was actually putting into effect an order for withdrawal which was to take his 19th Army back to the area Lyons–Aix-les-Bains. De Lattre did not know, and could not have known, that Wiese was getting ready to retreat. The risk he mentioned was a real one to him and had to be faced.

## Toulon and Marseilles liberated

The liberation of Toulon was completed on August 27 by the capitulation of Rear-Admiral Ruhfus, who had found a last refuge from the shells of the navy and the bombs of the air force in the Saint Mandrier peninsula. The assault on Toulon had cost the French 2,700 men killed and wounded, but they had taken over 17,000 prisoners and several hundred guns.

On August 23 de Lattre sent the 1st Armoured Division into Marseilles, and together with the 3rd Algerian Division and the Moroccan goums it overcame the resistance within the city. As in Toulon, the Germans defended themselves bitterly, using rocket launchers, mines, and flamethrowers. The loss successively of Notre Dame de la Garde and Fort Saint Nicolas, however, ended

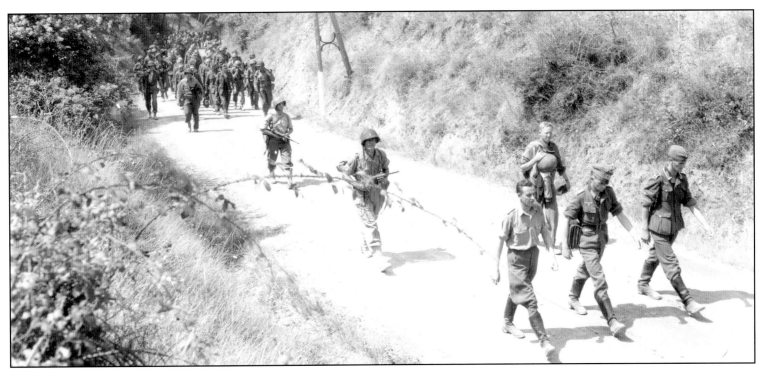

*Op Dragoon - 1st Abn, 7th US Army with German POW's.*

Schäffer's resistance and in the evening of the 27th he wrote to Monsabert:

"Prolonged resistance seems pointless in view of your superior strength. I ask you to cease firing from 2100 to 0800 hours so that surrender terms may be finalised for mid-day on the 28th and that I may have a decision from you which will allow me either to surrender with honour or to fight to the finish."

Neither General de Monsabert nor his commander were men to overlook the valour of the 244th Division. And so the armistice was signed on August 28 shortly before 0800 hours.

## Allied victory in Provence

The Allies were now a month ahead of schedule. The fury of their attacks had cost them 4,000 killed and wounded, but they had wiped out two enemy divisions and captured 37,000 prisoners.

Before ceasing all resistance the Germans blew up the port installations in Marseilles and Toulon. Until these were restored, the Provence beaches had landed 380,000 men, 69,312 vehicles, 306,000 tons of supplies and matériel, and 17,848 tons of fuel. By May 8, 1945, 905,512 men and 4,123,794 tons of matériel had passed through the hastily-reconstructed ports of Marseilles, Toulon, and Port de Bouc. These figures are taken from Morison, who claims, and we would agree with him, that for this alone Operation "Dragoon" was justified.

*1st Parachute brigade at Arnhem Bridge.*

General Bradley was to describe his stupefaction on learning of Operation "Market Garden" which Montgomery had got Eisenhower to approve and with which Bradley did not agree:

"Had the pious teetotaling Montgomery wobbled into S.H.A.E.F. with a hangover, I could not have been more astonished than I was by the daring adventure he proposed. For in contrast to the conservative tactics Montgomery ordinarily chose, the Arnhem attack was to be made over a 60-mile carpet of airborne troops. Although I never reconciled myself to the venture, I nevertheless freely concede that Monty's plan for Arnhem was one of the most imaginative of the war."

In effect the "carpet" over which XXX Corps was to advance towards the northern outskirts of Arnhem was 60 miles long and criss-crossed six times by canals and watercourses. Eisenhower had put at Montgomery's disposal the 1st Airborne Army. Commanded by U.S. Lieutenant-General L. H. Brereton, it engaged its I Airborne Corps (Lieutenant-General F. A. M. Browning) as follows:

1. U.S. 101st Airborne Division (Major-General Maxwell D. Taylor) would take Eindhoven by surprise and seize the bridges on the Wilhelmina Canal, the Dommel, and the Willems Canal;

2. U.S. 82nd Airborne Division (Major-General James M. Gavin) would take the Grave bridge over the Maas and the Nijmegen bridge over the Waal (the southern arm of the Rhine); and

3. British 1st Airborne Division (Major-General R. E. Urquhart) would take the bridges over the Neder Rijn (the northern arm of the Rhine) at Arnhem. It would then establish a bridgehead around the town and be reinforced by the Polish 1st Parachute Brigade, then by the British 52nd (Airportable) Division.

It was along the corridor opened up by these forces that the three divisions of the British XXX Corps (the Guards Armoured, the 43rd, and the 50th Divisions) under Horrocks were to advance towards Arnhem and, breaking out of the bridgehead, drive on at full speed to the Zuiderzee, a final run of about 37 miles.

## Allied Intelligence misses II Panzer Corps

All things considered, it does seem that Operation "Market Garden" relied heavily on what Frederick the Great called "Her Sacred Majesty Chance" and the expectation that she would favour Generals Browning and Horrocks for several days and under all circumstances. Even had she favoured them throughout, however, it is unlikely that XXX Corps could have made the run to Berlin all alone, as Eisenhower had no strategic reserves or logistic resources to exploit fully any initial success of this risky enterprise.

Yet XXX Corps' advance had to take place up a single road flanked by low-lying country, covered with a network of drainage ditches. This was to provide ideal terrain for the Germans to slow down or even halt the advance with a tenacious anti-tank defence, while launching flank attacks against XXX Corps' own communications. And this, in fact, was what was to happen.

Although Montgomery knew from intelligence reports that two Panzer divisions (part of the 11 S.S. Panzer Corps) were refitting just north of Arnhem, he believed them incapable of effective action and Horrocks, the commander of XXX Corps, was not even informed that these German forces lay so close to the battle area.

In fact, these forces also included the 1st Parachute Army which was being built up in the region of 's Hertogenbosch under the command of Colonel-General Kurt Student, the victor of Crete. The Allied forces, with their limited resources, had little chance of success. Additionally, it is arguable that the objectives of "Market Garden" were beyond the Allies' capabilities. The plan would clearly involve a great deal of risk

.

## Operation "Market Garden"

On Sunday September 17, 1944, zero hour struck at 1430. Under the near or distant cover of 1,200 fighters the first elements of Lieutenant-General Browning's three airborne divisions, which had been packed into 2,800 aircraft and 1,600 gliders, jumped or landed as close as possible to their objectives without undue losses.

For the 101st Airborne Division all went well, except for the Son bridge over the Wilhelmina Canal which it could not save from destruction. The 82nd managed to surprise the Grave bridge, but in the evening, when the Germans had got over the shock, it failed in its first attempt on Nijmegen. By this time General Student had got the plans for "Market Garden" which had been found on board an American glider shot down behind the German lines. Because of heavy A.A. fire round Arnhem it had been decided that the first echelon of the British 1st Airborne Division would drop in heath-land seven miles from the Neder

Rijn bridges. Moreover there were not enough aircraft to carry the whole division in one lift, so that three successive drops were necessary.

Field-Marshal Model, commander of Army Group "B" at Oosterbeek, alerted General Bittrich, commanding 11 S.S. Panzer Corps, and counter-attacked with the 9th "Hohenstaufen" Panzer Division through Arnhem and the 10th "Frundsberg" along the left bank of the Neder Rijn.

## The British outpaced

The British no longer had surprise, and now problems mounted as for technical and topographical reasons, their radio communications broke down. The divisional commander, Urquhart, decided to go up to the front himself, and within minutes he had lost all means of co-ordinating the movements of his division. Towards 2000 hours Lieutenant-Colonel Frost's battalion, whose commander had led the raid on Bruneval in 1942, had reached a point opposite the road bridge at Arnhem, but was almost surrounded.

Supported on the left by XII Corps and on the right by VIII Corps (Lieutenant-General Evelyn H. Baring), XXX Corps got off to a good start. Admirably supported, as its commander said, by No. 83 Group, Tactical Air Force (Air ViceMarshal H. Broadhurst), it reached Valkenswaard at the end of the day. A day later its Guards Armoured Division was at Son, where the bridge over the canal was repaired by dawn on the 19th. There was good contact with the 82nd Airborne Division, which had resumed its attack on Nijmegen, but without much success.

*Parartroopers with Short Stirling aircraft.*

By now it had begun to rain. "Market Garden", in fact, enjoyed only one day of blue skies out of ten. Were the weather forecasts ignored? There were consequential delays in the reinforcement of the airborne divisions and a notable drop in efficiency of the ground support. XXX Corps had only one axis along which to advance its 23,000 vehicles. During the 19th, Horrocks was able to get his tanks from Son to Nijmegen (36 miles), but it was not until the evening of the following day that the British and the Americans, fighting side by side, succeeded in crossing the Waal and seizing the road and rail bridges which Model had ordered to be left intact for a counter-attack.

When he had been given his orders the day before "Market Garden" was launched, Browning asked Montgomery how long he would have to hold the Arnhem bridge.

"Two days" said Monty briskly. "They'll be up with you by then."

"We can hold it for four." Browning replied. "But I think we might be going a bridge too far."

## The British driven back

The operation was now in its fifth day, and during the night of September 19–20 Urquhart had had to resign himself to abandoning Frost to his fate and to pulling his unit into the district of Oosterbeek with its back to the Neder Rijn. The bad weather continued, air supplies were reduced to practically nothing, and what was dropped fell equally amongst the Germans and the Allies. In the evening of the 21st, Lieutenant-Colonel Frost was seriously wounded and his battalion, now reduced to about 100 men, was captured by the Germans. On the 21st and 22nd the Polish 1st Parachute Brigade (Major-General Sosabowski) landed almost opposite Oosterbeek, whilst the Guards (Major-General Allan Adair) and the 43rd Division (Major-General Ivor Thomas) were caught in flank by the 10th "Frundsberg" S.S. Panzer Division as they tried to cover the ten miles between the Waal and the Neder Rijn. XXX Corps' forward positions, now sticking out like a finger in the German lines, risked being cut off at any moment from either east or west.

The survivors of the British 1st Airborne Division now received the order to pull back to the left bank of the Neder Rijn. 2,163 of them got across during the night of September 25–26 out of a total of 8,905 officers, N.C.O.s, and men and the 1,100 glider-pilots who had held off the attacks of II S.S. Panzer Corps for the last ten days. The Poles left behind 1,000 of their men and the U.S. 82nd and 101st Airborne Divisions lost respectively 1,669 and 2,074 killed, wounded, and missing. Between September 17 and 30, then, about one-third of the 34,876 men who fought between Eindhoven and Arnhem were lost. The people of Arnhem showed admirable devotion and courage in hiding 250 British paratroopers and helping them to escape: among these were Brigadiers J. W. Hackett and G. W. Lathbury.

## Major-General Urquhart's epic at Arnhem

In a letter dated September 28 and written in his own hand, Field-Marshal Montgomery expressed the admiration he felt at the bearing of Major-General Urquhart's division. Recalling the centuries-old roll-call of famous deeds by British arms, he wrote to him:

"There can be few episodes more glorious than the epic of Arnhem, and those that follow after will find it hard to live up to the high standards that you have set.

"So long as we have in the armies of the British Empire officers and men who will do as you have done, then we can indeed look forward with complete confidence to the future. In years to come it will be a great thing for a man to be able to say 'I fought at Arnhem!'"'

## "Market Garden" a failure

History will bear out this judgement. It is not certain, however, that it will also ratify Montgomery's conclusions on the glorious and tragic episode. In his opinion, if the success of the undertaking was not as great as had been expected, this was because the supply services, contrary to Eisenhower's orders, refused to cut down on rations for the American 3rd Army. General Bradley thought otherwise and wrote to the C.-in-C. on September 21: "… all plans for the future operations always lead back to the fact that in order to supply an operation of any size beyond the Rhine, the port of Antwerp is essential."

On September 4 the Scheldt estuary could have been cleared within a few days, and the rapidity of this success would have been a real shot in the arm to the Allied supply problem. Instead, the operation started on September 29 by the 21st Army Group dragged on for a whole month. By November 3 it was all over, but the Germans had profited from the delay by mining the canal, and clearing operations took another three weeks of dangerous and intensive work. Antwerp's major port facilities thus went unused from September 4 to November 23, whilst less than 90 miles away to the south-west the U.S. 1st Army was reduced to cutting down on petrol and ammunition. There were, of course, the "Red Ball Highways". The American historian Robert W. Merrian, writing of these roads, organised from August 25 onwards by Lieutenant-General J. C. H. Lee, says of the service:

"The Red Ball supply high road grew and grew, like Topsy, until it stretched over 700 well-marked miles, thoroughly equipped with fast wreckage and servicing stations manned twenty-four hours a day. The Red Ball began operating on August 25 with 5,400 vehicles, hauled a daily average of about 5,000 tons of supplies for the eighty-one days of its operation. On its peak day of operation, over 12,000 tons of supplies were hauled to the front, more than enough for twelve fighting divisions. Operating on a circle route, it was a vast one-way traffic circle, along which raced the life blood of the advancing troops. The driving was hard, the roads merciless on the vehicles, the turnover of equipment staggering, but the supplies were pushed through."

If Operation "Market Garden" proved Allied logistics to have been at fault, it also prejudiced the build-up of a 100-mile salient which was necessary to support Bradley's offensive towards Bonn and Cologne. As Bradley had feared, the British 2nd Army's northwards push ended up between Maastricht, Nijmegen, and Breda. When Antwerp finally got priority Bradley had had to

*German troops on the alert during the attack of Arnhem.*

lend two divisions temporarily to 21st Army Group to help in its capture.

Meanwhile the Canadian 1st Army had seized Le Havre (September 12), Boulogne (September 22), and Calais (October 1), capturing more than 28,000 prisoners. The combined effects of Allied bombardment and German destruction meant that it took longer than expected to get the ports working again. Le Havre in particular had had nearly 10,000 tons of bombs dropped on it and by late October was down to 15 per cent of its capacity. The day after the capture of Boulogne, however, the Allies were able to lay between this port and Dungeness a second 16-tube pipeline, which greatly alleviated the Allied petrol problem.

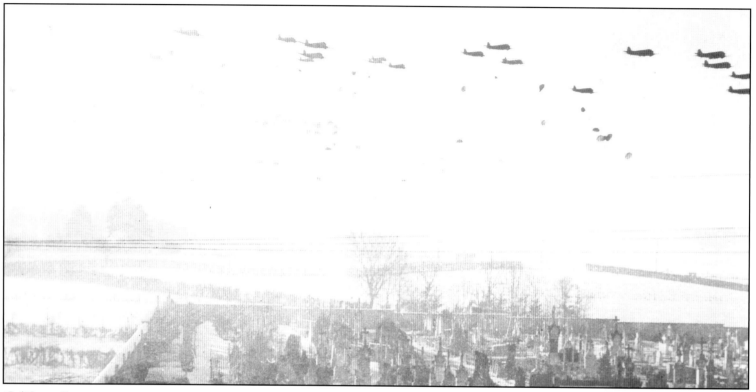

*C-47's over Bastogne.*

It was quite clear to Rundstedt, Model, and even to Sepp Dietrich, that the objectives assigned to Operation "Herbstnebel" ("Autumn Fog") were far too ambitious for the Wehrmacht's limited capabilities, and they tried to convince the Führer of this. On the other hand they agreed with him — and history bears out their judgement — that if the Third Reich was not to be annihilated in less than six months, they would have to go over to the offensive, the Western Front being the only theatre where this might be possible. Italy was not vital to the Western Allies, even if the terrain and the season had made such an operation there successful; and in the East, it was generally agreed that they would not be able to force a decisive result. According to Major-General Gehlen's calculations, Stalin had something like 520 infantry divisions and more than 300 armoured and mechanised brigades at his command, and so could lose up to 30 divisions, or retreat up to 150 miles, without suffering a decisive defeat. In any case, what could be the advantage to the Germans of advancing once more to the Dniepr or the Dvina, if in the meantime the Western Allies broke through the Westwall and occupied the Ruhr and Saar basins?

The German chiefs thus agreed unanimously on a counter-offensive in the West, being fully aware of the logistical difficulties and man-power shortage by which Eisenhower was being plagued. However, there was deep disagreement between the Filhrer and his front-line generals on how far to carry the offensive.

Hitler maintained that they ought to go all out, and inflict on Eisenhower a defeat as crushing as that suffered by Gamelin when the Panzer divisions had pushed through to the Somme estuary in 1940. And the fact that the Ardennes mountains were so lightly held seemed to provide him with an opportunity identical to the one he had exploited in May 1940 — we now know that he did in fact send to Liegnitz for the documents pertaining to "Fall Gelb". The plan was being prepared at H.Q. in absolute secrecy — and neither Rundstedt nor Model knew of it. Three armies were to take part: the newly formed 6th S.S. Panzerarmee, commanded by Colonel-General Dietrich; the 5th Panzerarmee under General Hasso von Manteuffel, which was withdrawn from the Aachen front (neither Model nor Rundstedt was informed of the rôle it was going to play); and the 7th Army, under General Brandenberger, which was then in the Eifel sector.

According to O.K.W.'s plan, the 5th and 6th Panzerarmee were to get to the Meuse in 48 hours; after this Sepp Dietrich, crossing the river north of Liège, would aim for Antwerp, via Saint Truiden and Aarschot, whilst Manteuffel, crossing the river on both sides of Namur, would aim for Brussels. The 7th Army would pivot round at Echternach and thus cover the operation against any Allied counter-attack coming from the south. With Manteuffel and Dietrich intercepting their communications at Namur and Antwerp, the whole of the Allied 21st Army Group, and most of the 12th Army Group, would be attacked on two fronts and annihilated, with the destruction of 37 of the 64 divisions that Eisenhower deployed at that time.

On October 24, Lieutenant-Generals Krebs and Westphal,

chiefs-of-staff of Army Group "B" and of O.B. West respectively, had an interview with the Führer, who informed them of the plan which he had conceived, and whose execution was provisionally fixed for November 25. Both at Koblenz and at Field-Marshal Model's H.Q., the Führerbefehl had been severely criticised by those who would have to carry it out, asand Krebs and Westphal had already hinted as much on a previous visit to O.K.W. — the plan bore no relationship to the resources being made available to them. Since, however, they were both in favour of a strategic counter-attack, on November 3 they submitted a counter-proposition to Hitler, better suited to the capabilities of Army Group "B", and called the "little solution" (kleine Lösung).

Hitler angrily rejected such a solution, for what he needed was not a short respite, but a decisive military victory in the West. So, as early as November 1, he had written at the head of his orders to O.B. West, that "the intention, the organisation, and the objective of this offensive are irrevocable". On receiving the counter-proposition of Model and Rundstedt, he got Jodl to reply within 24 hours that "the Führer has decided that the operation is irrevocably decided, down to its last details".

## Skorzeny's special forces

Among the special forces used during this operation, mention should be made of the so-called 150th Panzer Brigade, made up of about 2,000 men conversant with American army slang, using jeeps, and even old Sherman tanks rescued from the battlefield. The brigade had a double purpose: firstly, small patrols were to infiltrate the enemy lines and cause panic by spreading alarmist rumours and sabotaging telephone communications and signposts; then, when the breakthrough was being exploited, small motorised columns would be sent out to capture the Meuse bridges and hold them until the rest of the armour arrived.

This "Trojan horse" invented by Hitler was placed under the command of Otto Skorzeny. The stratagem, which was quite contrary to the Geneva Convention, had some initial success because of its surprise element, but the counter-measures immediately devised by the Americans were most effective. Germans captured in American uniforms were immediately tried and shot, although some of them had only taken part in the operation when threatened with a German firing-squad.

The paratroops who spread confusion deep behind the American front line, even as far as France, never numbered more than 1,200, discounting the dummies used, and were commanded by Lieutenant-Colonel Heydte; but the pilots of the Junkers Ju 52s from which they were to jump were so badly trained that three-quarters of them jumped behind the German lines. The Allies thought they had been entrusted with the task of ki

## Inadequate reserves

Behind the first wave of troops, there were eight reserve divisions, seven of which were subject to O.K.W. orders. Model thus found himself with very little chance of exploiting any slight advantages he might gain without referring to Hitler. In addition there were two newly formed Panzer brigades; but that was all.

Theoretically, the attack was to be supported by 3,000 bombers and fighter-bombers, but on the first day a mere 325

planes took off, of which 80 were jets. Hitler could not bring himself to expose German towns to Allied air attacks by depriving them of fighter cover.

On the first day of the offensive, the 6th S.S. Panzerarmee attacked with its infantry divisions, keeping its Panzers in reserve to exploit the initial success. On the right it came up against the American 2nd and 99th Divisions, of V Corps, still commanded by Major-General Leonard Gerow; the 2nd Division was an experienced, battle-hardened unit which overcame its surprise very quickly, whereas the 99th Division, which had never before seen major action, had more difficulty in recovering its composure. In the end, V Corps managed to hold on to the Elsenborn ridge in spite of all enemy attacks. But Dietrich easily broke through the Losheim gap, lightly held by the 14th Armoured Division, which opened up the road to Stavelot, and in addition enabled him to turn the left flank of the 106th Division.

On the very same day this division was pierced on its left by the 5th Panzerarmee's attack, which also threw back the 28th Division towards Clervaux (Clerf). The two regiments of the 106th Division holding the Schnee Eifel plateau were in imminent danger of being surrounded.

The 7th Army, reduced to four divisions, had to be satisfied with pivoting around Echternach, instead of including Luxembourg in its plan of attack, as originally planned. Although it had to yield some ground, the American 4th Division, which made up Middleton's right flank, was less severely tested than the 28th.

## The Allied response

When the first news of the German attack reached S.H.A.E.F., Bradley was in Versailles, conferring with General Bedell Smith, Eisenhower's chief-of-staff. A few hours later, a further report indicated that the American 1st Army had identified eight German divisions.

Eisenhower and Bradley immediately realised the implications of this offensive, but the reserves available to them on December 16 were even less than those available to General Gamelin on May 13, 1940. They were in fact limited to XVIII Airborne Corps (Major-General Ridgeway), two of whose divisions, the 82nd and the 101st, were being reformed near Rheims, after two months' action in the Nijmegen salient. This corps was immediately alerted, and the 9th and 3rd Armies received orders to make their 7th and 10th Armoured Divisions respectively available to the 1st Army.

In a few days' time Eisenhower would also be able to call upon the 2nd Armoured Division, which had just landed in France, as well as the 87th Division and the 17th Airborne Division, which were still in England, but about to embark for France. Even then it would take time for them to come into the line, In addition, although the successes of Skorzeny's commandos and von der Heydte's paratroopers were very slight, rumour greatly magnified them. Above all, the bad weather of that week reduced Allied air strikes almost to nothing. But "low cloud" and "thick fog" were phrases that the weather forecasters repeated with monotonous regularity throughout the week December 16–23.

*German PzKpfw V passes army truck.*

## The Germans waver

In the public mind the Ardennes campaign is summed up in the one word: Bastogne, and rightly so, since Brigadier-General A. C. McAuliffe and his 101st Airborne Division fought heroically around the little town, although the behaviour under fire of the 7th Armoured Division and its commander, Brigadier-General Robert Hasbrook, was also worthy of the highest praise. Between December 18 and 22, the defensive position of Saint Vith compelled the 5th Panzerarmee to disperse its energies, and the town was only evacuated after an express order.

It is true that on December 19, in the Schnee Eifel plateau region, two regiments of the 106th Division were trapped, and

*Generals of the 101st Airborne Division Bastogne, Belgium.*

6,000 men had to surrender, but everywhere else the Americans stood up gallantly under all the attacks.

On the German side, Dietrich made the big mistake of stubbornly trying to take the Elsenborn ridge, whose defences had been greatly strengthened by the transfer to General Gerow of that first-class fighting unit, the American 1st Division; thus the 12th "Hitlerjugend" S.S. Panzer Division was halted around Bütgenbach. As for the celebrated "Leibstandarte", it became separated from its advanced elements, which had pushed forward into the Amblève valley, on Colonel Peiper's orders. In short, four days after the initial attack, the 6th Panzerarmee was still far from the Meuse bridges — which it should have reached within 72 hours.

## Bastogne reached

While Dietrich wasted time in attempts to secure the

Elsenborn Ridge, Manteuffel displayed more tactical flair. The latter received further help from the fact that General Hodges found it more difficult to reinforce his VIII Corps' elements in Luxembourg than those between Elsenborn and Trois-Points: Clervaux and Wiltz fell easily, and the way to Bastogne was opened up. Faced with this most unexpected development — for after all, it had been thought that Dietrich's force: would have the starring rôle in this offensive — Model and Rundstedt recommended the immediate transfer of II S.S. Panzer Corps from the 5th to the 6th Panzerarmee, following the principle that successful operations ought to be exploited in preference to the less successful.

But Hitler refused categorically to allow this transfer; no doubt because he dreaded admitting, even implicitly, the failure of Dietrich and the Waffen-S.S., and did not want to place one of the Nazi Party's armed units under the command of the Wehrmacht generals for whom for a long time he felt nothing but mistrust, and even hate.

Had Eisenhower known that his adversary was making this tactical mistake, he would probably have refrained from taking some of the measures which marked his intervention on December 19. But with all his reports from the front indicating that Bastogne and the 101st Airborne Division were practically surrounded, he decided that the time had come to throw all his authority into the struggle. So, at 1100 hours on December 19, he convened a meeting with Bradley and Devers, together with Patton.

According to his memoirs, Eisenhower opened the meeting

by declaring that "the present situation is to be regarded as one of opportunity for us and not disaster. There will be only cheerful faces at this conference table."

And in fact these confident phrases represented exactly the calm coolness that Eisenhower really felt on that important day. The main decision taken was to move the six divisions of General Patton's III and XII Corps from the Saar front to the Echternach–Diekirch–Bastogne front, at the same time subordinating VIII Corps to the 3rd Army. This meant that the right flank of General Devers's army group would be extended from Bitche to Saarbrücken. Such a manoeuvre had already been discussed at 3rd Army H.Q., so that a single telephone call made from Verdun by its commander was enough to get it started. According to Farago, this order, which meant the moving of 133,178 vehicles over a total of some 1,500,000 miles, was carried out in five days. During this time, the 3rd Army's rear echelons transported 62,000 tons of supplies, the Intelligence staff distributed thousands of maps of the new sector, and the communications section put down 40,000 yards of telephone cable. And all this was achieved in snow and on roads covered with black ice. This proves that Patton may have been a swashbuckler (that very day he said to Bradley: "'Brad, this time the Kraut's stuck his head in the meatgrinder.' With a turn of his fist he added, 'And this time I've got hold of the handle.'"), but he was also a thinker, and an organiser of the highest class. This combination of intellect and dash made Patton unique.

## "Act aggressively with our full capabilities"

On December 20, Eisenhower placed Montgomery in charge of the northern flank of the German penetration (with the U.S. 1st and 9th armies under his command), and gave Bradley the southern flank. As he reported to the Combined Chiefs-of-Staff: with the enemy thrusting towards Namur, "our front is divided into two main parts on each of which we must act aggressively and with our full capabilities."

## Bastogne hangs on

On the morning of December 19, the 101st Division entered Bastogne, joining up with those elements of the 9th and 10th Armoured Divisions defending the town. The next day, XLVII Panzer Corps, following its instructions, bypassed the town to north and south, leaving the 26th Volksgrenadier Division the job of laying siege to it. When the commander of this formation, Lieutenant-General Heinz Kokott, called upon General McAuliffe to surrender, he received the rudest of replies: "Nuts". The garrison's high morale was kept up, firstly, by the wholehearted support of the town population under their mayor, Monsieur Jacmin, and secondly by the sound of III Corps' guns announcing the beginning of the counter-attack in the south.

On the northern half of the bulge, an attack by the 30th Division, called by the Germans "Roosevelt's S.S.", enabled Hodges to close up the Amblève valley sector by lengthening the position held by V Corps. However, by sending in II S.S. Panzer Corps to the left of I S.S. Panzer Corps, Dietrich succeeded in revitalising the offensive, forcing Hasbrook to evacuate Saint Vith on December 21. The intervention, firstly of XVIII Airborne

Corps (although reduced to the 82nd Airborne Division), and secondly, of General Collins's VII Corps, comprising the 75th, 83rd, and 84th Divisions, and the 3rd Armoured Division, enabled a continuous front to be re-established on a line Manhay–Grandmenil–Hotton–Marche.

By December 22, at Koblenz, Rundstedt had decided upon immediate withdrawal from the engagement, already running into trouble. Of course, Hitler, at Ziegenberg, refused to ratify this suggestion; he thought that if they threw in the O.K.W. reserves, especially the 9th Panzer and 3rd and 15th Panzergrenadier Divisions, they would be able to resume the offensive, or at least capture Bastogne, the main thorn in their side.

## Allied air power to the fore

On December 23, an anti-cyclone brought with it a week of brilliant sunshine over the whole of the Ardennes front. The Allied air forces were immediately unleashed, flying 2,000 missions on the first day, and 15,000 in the next three days. On Christmas Eve, at a cost of 39 planes lost, 2,000 American bombers, escorted by 900 fighters, attacked the airfields near Frankfurt and the communications networks of Kaiserslautern, Bad Munster, Koblenz, Neuwied, and Euskirchen. At the same time, other air attacks were successfully launched on the enemy's rear and on certain battlefield objectives. Last, but not least, 961 Dakotas and 61 gliders were able to drop 850 tons of supplies and ammunition to beleaguered Bastogne.

This movement laid bare Patton's left flank, and Eisenhower transferred to the 3rd Army the 87th Division, the 11th

Armoured Division, and the 17th Airborne Division. Thus, by December 24, 32 Allied divisions were in action or in reserve on the Ardennes front, against 29 German divisions calculated by S.H.A.E.F. to be involved.

## 2nd Panzer Division wiped out

Faced with this further deterioration of the situation, Rundstedt renewed his plea that the offensive be abandoned. He was very strongly supported this time by General Guderian, who knew that in the East, Soviet forces were massing on the Vistula bridge-heads. Once again the Führer refused categorically, in spite of the arguments of his H.Q., only too aware of the disasters that his obstinacy would inevitably bring. In the meantime Lieutenant-General von Lauchert's 2nd Panzer Division had reached Ciney, Beauraing, and Celles, in contact with the British 29th Armoured Brigade, and only six miles from the Meuse at Dinant. On Christmas Day, it suffered a flank attack at the hands of the American 2nd Armoured Division (Major-General Harmon), which had just been transferred to VII Corps. The effect was one of total surprise, and the disaster was no less complete. By the end of the day, Lauchert's losses were as follows: 1,050 prisoners, 2,500 killed, 81 tanks (out of a total of 88), seven assault guns, all his artillery (74 pieces), and 405 vehicles. That day the American 2nd Armoured Division certainly lived up to its nickname of "Hell on Wheels". Confronted with this crushing blow, Manteuffel could only withdraw his XLVII Panzer Corps to Rochefort.

## Patton relieves Bastogne

Patton's 3rd Army had a little more difficulty in relieving Bastogne, as the German 5th Parachute Division under Lieutenant-General Hellmann, on the right of the German 7th Army, put up a very spirited resistance. It was not until December 26 that the American 4th Armoured Division under Major-General Gaffey managed to link up with the beleaguered garrison, and even then it was only by means of a narrow corridor a few hundred yards wide.

## Half-success into defeat

Faced with these defeats, Hitler dis engaged.  He would have been far better advised to have taken his head out of the "meatgrinder", when the results were in his favour. However, instead of rapidly withdrawing his 5th and 6th Panzerarmee behind the Westwall, he insisted on their trying to hold the Ardennes salient in impossible conditions, so turning his half-success of December 16 into a clear failure. That this is so is clear from the losses of the two sides: in manpower the Americans had suffered 76,890 casualties to the Germans' 81,834; in tanks 733 to 324; and aircraft 592 to 320. Whereas the Americans could replace their matériel losses with little difficulty, the Germans could not.

When one realises that German possibilities of rebuilding the Wehrmacht's strength were slowly diminishing, and that on January 12, 1945 Stalin unleashed his fifth and last winter offensive, there is no doubt that these figures confirm the German defeat, not only in the Ardennes, but on the whole of the Western

*German soldiers by captured US equipment.*

Front. To the despair of Guderian the abandonment of Operation "Herbstnebel" did not mean a reinforcement of the Eastern Front forces, for Hitler saw "Herbstnebel" as only the first of a set of offensives in the West. The first, aimed at the recovery of Alsace and Lorraine, was propounded by Hitler to his generals on December '18. "Our first objective", he said, "must be to clean up the situation in the West by offensive action."

In this mood of total fantasy, Germany's Supreme Commander brought in the New Year, 1945.

*Trucks carrying US troops advance through Speicher.*

On March 8, 1945, Field-Marshal Kesselring was ordered to leave the Italian theatre of operations immediately and go to an audience with the Führer. The following afternoon, Hitler told him that as a result of the unfortunate situation at Remagen, he had decided to make him Commander-in-Chief in the West. Hitler had spent several hours discussing with Kesselring, first alone, later in the company of Keitel and Jodl. On the whole, Hitler was optimistic about the future. He thought that a collapse in the East would be the end of the war, but he had provided for this eventuality and added, according to Kesselring's notes taken immediately after the audience: "our main military effort is directed to the East. He [Hitler] envisages the decisive battle there, with complete confidence. And he expects the enemy's main attack to be launched at Berlin."

For this reason the 9th Army, which was charged with the defence of the city, had been given priority consideration. So there were grounds for assurance that the Berlin front would not be broken; similarly with Army Group "Centre", on the borders of Silesia and Czechoslovakia, which had gained notable successes. Its commander, Schörner, assured Hitler that "with reinforcements and sufficient supplies, he would repel all enemy attacks launched at him".

As regards the situation on the Western Front, the heavy losses sustained by the British, Americans, and French over months of heavy fighting were a factor that should be taken into account. Furthermore, in Hitler's opinion, "the Allies could not dismiss the natural obstacles covering the German Army's positions. The Allied bridgehead at Remagen was the danger point and it was urgent it should be mopped up; but there too Hitler was confident."

In these conditions, Kesselring's task was to hold on long enough for the Eastern Front armies to be brought up to strength, so that O.K.W. could then despatch the necessary reinforcements to the armies in the West. Within a short while, the deficiencies of the Luftwaffe, held to blame for the failures of recent months, would be forgotten and Grand-Admiral Dönitz's new submarines would have turned the tables in the Battle of the Atlantic, bringing much needed relief to the defence of the Third Reich. d Waiting for the big day: Allied supplies under camouflage by the side of a road leading to the Rhine and the heart of Germany.

## Kesselring caught off balance

Thus armed with encouragement, Kesselring received his chief-of-staff's report in the night of March 9–10 at the H.Q. at Ziegenberg just vacated by Rundstedt. General Westphal had been his chief-of-staff, during his time as supreme commander in Italy, and Kesselring had complete confidence in him.

The new commander must have been considerably shocked by the unembroidered account of the situation that he received. With 55 battle-worn divisions giving him, on average, a coverage of 63 fighting men for each mile of the front, it was his task to hold 85 full strength Allied divisions, which also enjoyed all the benefits of undisputed air superiority.

On March 11, at the H.Q. of LIII Corps, Kesselring met Field-Marshal Model and General von Zangen, commanding the 15th Army, which had been given the job of wiping out the Remagen bridgehead. All were agreed that this objective could not be attained unless there was considerable speeding up in the supply of substantial reinforcements, and above all of ammunition, and this filled Kesselring with apprehension. The morale of Army Group "H" gave him some comfort, however, especially since the enemy attack across the lower Rhine was taking time in getting under way. On the other hand, the position of Army Group "G", without any mobile reserves worthy of the name, seemed fraught with risk.

Hence Kesselring was not so much caught unawares as off guard by Operation "Undertone", the American offensive south of the Moselle, which he learnt had been launched when he returned from this rapid tour of inspection. The series of attacks by the American generals came as a disagreeable revelation to the Germans. In the face of this violent American thrust, O.B. West appealed to O.K.W. for authorisation to withdraw the German 1st and 7th Armies to the right bank of the Rhine; typically, Hitler procrastinated until it was too late to accept this eminently reasonable course. And the only reinforcement destined for the Western Front was a single division, which was not even combat-worthy as it had spent some considerable time in Denmark on garrison duties. To cap this, Kesselring was informed of the surprise attack at Oppenheim, while the 1st Parachute Army brought news that north of the Ruhr, smokescreens maintained over several hours showed that Montgomery was putting the final touches to his careful preparations.

## Scorched earth policy

Kesselring felt no scruples in giving his support to Albert Speer, Reich Minister for Armaments and War Production, who was doing all he could to sabotage the execution of the "scorched earth" order promulgated by Hitler on March 19, 1945.

In setting out its motives, the monstrous Führerbefehl used the following line of argument:

"The fight for the existence of our people obliges us to make total use, even within the Reich, of whatever means may weaken the fighting power of the enemy and prevent him from pursuing his advance. Any means capable, directly or indirectly, of inflicting lasting damage on the offensive strength of the enemy must be resorted to. It is erroneous to think that by leaving them intact or with only superficial damage, we may more profitably resume exploitation of our communication and transport systems and our industrial or productive installations when we reconquer our invaded territory. When the enemy comes to retreat, he will have no consideration for the population, and will leave only scorched earth behind him."

So Hitler joined Morgenthau, whereas even Churchill and Roosevelt had rejected the inhuman and demented notion of "pastoralising" the German people. Albert Speer, however, devoted his entire energies to opposing the implementation of this insane order. Speer did not limit his opposition merely to pious utterances. He put the enormous weight of influence he had as dictator of industrial production to the task of avoiding implementation of the "scorched earth" order.

In this covert activity he received positive support from Kesselring; as a result, in its retreat from the Rhine to the Elbe and beyond, the German Army restricted itself to forms of destruction which are common in such cases to all the armies in the world.

## Montgomery prepares to cross the Rhine

On March 23, at 1530 hours, under a clear sky and with a favourable weather forecast, Montgomery launched Operation "Plunder/Varsity" and addressed the American, British, and Canadian troops under his command with an order of the day "21 ARMY GROUP WILL NOW CROSS THE RHINE."

Under his command he had two armies, eight corps, and 27 divisions (17 infantry, eight armoured, and two airborne; or, in national terms, 13 American, 12 British, and two Canadian). To these should be added the equivalent of three divisions represented

by five armoured brigades, a British commando brigade, and the Canadian 9th Infantry Brigade.

The British 2nd Army's attack, supplemented by the Canadian II Corps, was prepared for and supported by 1,300 pieces of artillery, with 600 guns fulfilling the same function for XVI Corps, which was to open the right bank of the Rhine for the American 9th Army. Such concentration of firepower necessitated the transport and dumping of 60,000 tons of ammunition. Massive area bombing by the Allied air forces extended the artillery action to German rail and road communications, isolating the battlefield. Between March 20 and 22, R.A.F. Bomber Command and the U.S. 8th and 9th Air Forces made 16,000 sorties over the area in question and dropped 49,500 tons of bombs (including 22,000-lb "Grand Slams"). Special attacks were launched on airfields where the Luftwaffe's new jet aircraft were stationed.

To build bridges across the Rhine, 30,000 tons of engineering equipment and 59,000 engineers had to be transported to the area. But before the construction required by Operation "Plunder" could be used, divisions in the first line of attack had to be conveyed from one bank to the other by other means. This task was carried out by a detachment of the Royal Navy, which left Antwerp to reach its departure point by a series of Belgian, Dutch, and German canals. It comprised 45 landing craft (L.C.M.), plus a formation of the 12-ton amphibious tanks known by the British as Buffaloes and as Alligators by the Americans. Preparations on this scale were obviously observable by the enemy, but the final deployment of the Allied forces was concealed by the smokescreen which hid the left bank of the Rhine over a distance of 75 miles between dawn on March 21 and 1700 hours on March 23.

On the right bank of the Rhine, the 1st Parachute Army was deployed with its right slightly upstream of Emmerich and its left in the region of Duisburg. It was thus defending a front of 45 miles with seven weak and, by now, worn-out divisions, but nonetheless, an adequate concentration for defence bearing in mind the natural obstacle of the broad river, had the divisions been at full complement. During the relative lull following March 11, they had dug themselves in well and the rapid construction of their defensive positions was entirely satisfactory to Kesselring. O.K.W. and O.B. West confidently expected an airborne landing. Accordingly, an entire anti-aircraft corps was put at the disposal of Blaskowitz, who deployed batteries all over the area between Munster and the right bank of the Rhine. But apparently to little effect: as on previous occasions the German soldier had to put up with implacable and practically unchallenged machine gun and cannon fire and bombing from Allied aircraft without seeing any fighters of his own in the sky.

## The battle begins

At 1700 hours on March 23, the smokescreen vanished and the entire artillery of the British 2nd Army and the American 9th Army opened fire on the enemy positions, maintaining their barrage of shells of all calibres until 0945 hours the following morning. This was, however, interspersed with pauses at times varying from sector to sector to allow the divisions launching the attack to feel out the enemy strength.

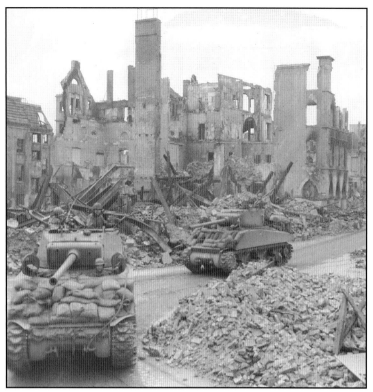

*Allied troops advance through Muenster.*

The main action devolved upon the British 2nd Army, in position north of the Lippe. On its left, XXX Corps had during the night got four battalions of the 51st Division (Major-General Thomas Rennie) across the Rhine; on its right, XII Corps had established its 15th Division (Major-General Colin Muir Barber) on the right bank of the river, opposite Xanten, while the 1st Commando Brigade went into action against the 180th Division in the ruins of Wesel. Further south, the American 9th Army, whose task was to cover the flank of the British attack, engaged its XVI Corps, whose 30th and 79th Divisions crossed the Rhine to either side of Rheinberg. According to Montgomery, German resistance was only sporadic, and certainly the two

*Knocked out Panzer Mk VIB "King Tiger".*

## Airborne landings

However, at 1000 hours the "event", in the Napoleonic sense of the word, took place. In the German camp, remembering the precedent of Arnhem, the Allies' airborne troops were expected to attack at the time that Montgomery's infantry was attempting to cross the Rhine, and to drop to the rear of the battlefield to effect a vertical encirclement of the 1st Parachute Army. But their attack came three hours after it had been anticipated, and the drop took place in the region of Hamminkeln, barely five miles from the right bank of the river. Under the command of Lieutenant-General Matthew B. Ridgway, XVIII Airborne Corps comprised the British 6th Airborne (Major-General E. Bols) and the American 17th Airborne (Major-General William E. Miley) Divisions, their transport being undertaken by 1,572 planes and 1,326 gliders, under close escort from 889 fighters. The 6th Airborne Division took off from 11 airfields in the south-east of England, the American 17th from 17 that had just been built in the area bounded by Rheims, Orléans, Evreux, and Amiens. The effect of surprise was so great and the German flak so well neutralised by Allied artillery pounding from the left bank that losses on landing amounted to no more than 46 transport planes and three per cent of the glider force employed in this operation, known as "Varsity".

The British and Americans fell on the enemy battery positions and reduced a good many of them to silence, then thrust on across the Diersforterwald to meet XII Corps, whose advance was strongly supported by 580 heavy guns of the 2nd Army, responding to calls for fire cover with most admirable speed and

American divisions mentioned above suffered only 31 killed in the enterprise.

The offensive undertaken by the 21st Army Group was no surprise for Blaskowitz, who had even correctly estimated its main point of impact and line of advance. Accordingly — and with a degree of haste for which Kesselring reproached him — he judged it opportune to throw in his armoured reserves. The dawn saw furious counter-attacks. In the course of the fighting between XXX Corps and the 15th Panzergrenadier Division, which brought into the line the paratroops from the German 6th and 7th Parachute Divisions, Major-General Rennie was killed, evidence enough of the enemy's determination.

precision.

At the end of the day, XVIII Airborne Corps made contact with the British XII Corps. Furthermore, thanks to units flown in by glider, XVIII Airborne Corps had taken intact a number of bridges over the IJssel which, flowing as it does parallel to the Rhine between Wesel and Emmerich, could have constituted an obstacle to the rapid exploitation of the day's successes. Moreover, the 84th Division was taken in rear and as good as annihilated, with the loss of most of the 3,789 prisoners counted by General Ridgway's Intelligence services.

## Large bridgehead

As night fell, in the zone between Dinslaken and Rees, where resistance from German parachute troops had lost none of its spirit, the 21st Army Group had taken a bridgehead 30 miles wide on the right bank of the Rhine, running, in the British XII Corps' (Lieutenant-General Sir Neil Methuen Ritchie) sector to a depth of nearly eight miles; the Allied bridge builders were free to get to work without any threat of retaliation on the part of enemy artillery. Montgomery could feel all the more satisfaction with the way things had gone on March 24 as he had committed only four of his eight corps.

## Collapse of the German 15th Army

On March 25 and 28, two further events of comparable scale and importance took place on the 12th Army Group's front: firstly, the collapse of the German 15th Army, whose task it was to contain the enemy within the Remagen bridgehead; and secondly,

adding its effect to the clean breakthrough by the American 1st Army, the crossing of the Main at the Aschaffenburg and Hanau bridges by the American 3rd Army.

## The Ruhr pocket

On March 25, the American 1st Army began its fresh offensive by smashing LXXIV Corps in the region of Breitscheid. Hodges immediately unleashed his 3rd, 7th, and 9th Armoured Divisions, which reached Giessen and Marburg on the 28th, 53 and 66 miles respectively from the Rhine at Neuwied. On the same day, in the 3rd Army, VIII Corps completed the mopping up of Frankfurt and made contact with Hodges's right in the region of Wiesbaden, thus trapping the enemy elements left on the right bank of the Rhine between the Lahn and the Main. But most strikingly, Patton's 4th, 6th, and 11th Armoured Divisions, in formation ahead of XII and XX Corps, had moved from the Main valley into that of the Fulda, making in the direction of Kassel. Thus Hodges, whose task was to reach the eastern outlets of the Ruhr basin, found himself provided with cover, just as Bradley intended, against a counterattack striking from the Harz mountains.

On the day after the surprise breakthrough at Oppenheim, Kesselring, according to his own account, had wondered "whether it was not best to accept the army groups' proposals and withdraw the entire front from the Rhine. I finally refrained from doing so, because the only result would have been to retreat in disorder."

Quite clearly, at the point reached in the German camp on March 28, Kesselring's conclusions were still more justified.

This was all the more true as the sappers of the 21st Army

Group had by March 26 opened seven 40-ton bridges to traffic, and the American 9th Army and British 2nd Army came down both banks of the Lippe to overwhelm the 1st Parachute Army. Two days later, on the left bank of this river, Lieutenant-General Simpson had his 8th Armoured Division (Major-General J. M. Devine) in the region of Haltern, more than 25 miles east of the Rhine. At the same time, Sir Miles Dempsey pushed the Guards Armoured Division (Major-General Allan Adair) down the Münster road, while his XXX and Canadian II Corps, on a line linking Borken–Bocholt–Isselburg–Emmerich, reached the Dutch frontier. The 1st Parachute Army was helplessly cut off, and its LXIII Corps and XLVII Panzer Corps (five divisions) were thrown back onto Army Group "B". And Montgomery poured his armoured units resolutely into the breach.

On April 2, 1945, as the day closed, the inevitable happened. The American 3rd Armoured Division, driving ahead of VII Corps (1st Army), met up at Lippstatt with the 8th Armoured Division coming from Haltern. In the course of this fighting, Major-General Rose, commanding the 3rd Armoured Division in its finest foray, was killed. Now Army Group "B" was encircled, with the exception of LXVII Corps, which had been attached to Army Group "B" following the breakthrough at Breitscheid.

Including the ruins of the 1st Parachute Army mentioned above, there were the 5th Panzerarmee and the 15th Army, of seven corps or 19 divisions (three of them Panzer, and the 3rd Panzergrenadier Division) caught in a trap that Hitler was quick to qualify as "the fortified region of the Ruhr". To reduce it, General Bradley formed a new 15th Army, under the command of Lieutenant-General Leonard T. Gerow, with a strength of five corps, including the newly-formed XXII and XXIII Corps, in all 18 divisions taken from the 1st and 9th Armies.

The encirclement of the Ruhr meant not only the rapid destruction of Army Group "B", but more importantly, the end of all organised resistance on the part of the Wehrmacht between Würzburg on the Main and Minden on the Weser. Between the inside of the wings of Army Groups "G" and "H", a breach of more than 180 miles was opened. It was too late for the unfortunate Kesselring to cherish the notion of repositioning his armies on a line along the courses of the Weser, Werra, Main, Altmuhl, and Lech, as favoured by 18th Century strategists.

## Eisenhower gives up the idea of Berlin …

To stop this breach, O.K.W. still had, in the Harz mountains, the 11th Army, comprising five divisions under the command of General Wenck, and a 12th Army being formed on the right bank of the Elbe. But clearly the way to Berlin lay open to the 12th Army Group and on April 4 S.H.A.E.F. transferred it to the American 9th Army, to the great satisfaction of General Simpson, its commander, and even more so of General Bradley, who saw the forces under his command now rise to four armies (11 corps of 48 divisions, 14 of them armoured, with some 3,600 tanks). But Eisenhower had no intention of giving Bradley the German capital as an objective. The question had already been considered by him among other options open to him after the encirclement of the Ruhr, and he had decided against going for Berlin for strategic and logistic reasons-in particular the lengthening of his lines of communication that this would entail, and the obstacle of the Elbe, something short of 200 miles from the Rhine and 125 from Berlin.

As a result of this decision, Eisenhower set himself the following objectives:

1. to make contact without delay with the Soviet forces moving west, and thus make it impossible for the enemy to try to regroup;

2. to hurl the 21st Army Group to the north-east, its right wing keeping its objective steadily fixed on Lübeck, to cut off the Wehrmacht forces occupying Norway and Denmark; and

3. for the 12th and 6th Army Groups, Eisenhower writes:

"Equally important was the desirability of penetrating and destroying the so-called 'National Redoubt'. For many weeks we had been receiving reports that the Nazi intention, in extremity, was to withdraw the cream of the S.S., Gestapo, and other organisations fanatically devoted to Hitler, into the mountains of southern Bavaria, western Austria, and northern Italy. There they expected to block the tortuous mountain passes and to hold out indefinitely against the Allies. Such a stronghold could always be reduced by eventual starvation if in no other way. But if the German was permitted to establish the redoubt he might possibly force us to engage in a long-drawn-out guerrilla type of warfare, or a costly siege. Thus he could keep alive his desperate hope that through disagreement among the Allies he might yet be able to secure terms more favourable than those of unconditional surrender. The evidence was clear that the Nazi intended to make the attempt and I decided to give him no opportunity to carry it out."

So, with the Elbe reached in the vicinity of Magdeburg, it was understood that Bradley would make his main line of advance along a line Erfurt-Leipzig–Dresden, with a secondary thrust on Regensburg and Linz. Contact would be made with the Russians in Saxony, and at the same time a march would be stolen on Army Group "G" in its task of occupying the redoubt. However logical this line of argument was from a strategic point of view, it rested on a hypothesis which was shown to be false after Germany's capitulation: the "national redoubt" concept was no more than a figment of the imagination of those who fed it to S.H.A.E.F.'s Intelligence services.

## Stalin approves warmly

In any event, on March 24, in accordance with a decision taken at the Yalta Conference, Eisenhower communicated his plan, summarised above, to Stalin who approved it most warmly. In the terms of a telegram cited in Churchill's memoirs but absent from Crusade in Europe, Stalin assured Eisenhower that his plan "entirely coincides with the plan of the Soviet High Command… Berlin has lost its former strategic importance. The Soviet High Command therefore plans to allot secondary forces in the direction of Berlin." Knowing as we do that at the very moment these lines were dictated, Stalin was concentrating five tank armies and 25,000 guns (expending 25,600 tons of shell) on an allegedly secondary objective, one sees what was in the wind.

*German soldier cries by his gun following his capture by Soviet troops.*

One of General Bradley's tasks was to reduce the "fortified area of the Ruhr" where, on Hitler's orders, Field-Marshal Model had shut himself in. Given the job of carrying out the operation, the American 15th Army attacked southwards across the Ruhr and westwards across the Sieg.

By April 12, Lieutenant-General Gerow had occupied the entire coal basin in which, despite the Führerbefehl of March 19, the Germans had done nothing to add to the destruction wrought by British and American bombing. Two days later, the pocket had been cut in two from north to south. In these conditions, Colonel-General Harpe, commanding the 5th Panzerarmee, recognising the fact that his chief had disappeared, ordered Army Group "B" to cease fighting. Capitulation delivered 325,000 prisoners (including 29 generals) into Allied hands. A vain search was instituted for Field-Marshal Walther Model, and it was learnt only four months later that he had committed suicide on April 21, lest he be handed over to the Russians after his surrender, and had been buried in a forest near Wuppertal.

Without waiting for the outcome here, the American 9th, 1st, and 3rd Armies exploited their advance to the full. Resistance grew weaker every day, and the average daily haul of prisoners rose from 10,600 between February 22 and March 31 to 29,000 for the week April 2 to 9, and reached 50,000 in the middle of the month. Evidently, the Landser (German "Tommy") was at the end of his tether, in spite of the growing wave of drumhead courts martial and summary executions. In the heart of the Reich, the multiplication of divisions went on almost to the final day, but whether they belonged to the Wehrmacht or to the Waffen-S.S., these new divisions, Volksgrenadier for the most part, revealed the paucity of their training as soon as they came under fire.

The Volkssturm, which was intended to fill the gaps in defence, was a pitiful ragbag of middle-aged men and adolescents, armed and equipped with any weapon that came to hand. In these conditions, allowing for sporadic but short-lived retaliation here and there from a few units that still retained some semblance of order and strength, the advance of the 12th Army Group across Germany gathered speed and took on more and more the character of a route march, facilitated by the Autobahn system, which in by-passing the towns removed inevitable bottlenecks. As a result, American losses dropped to insignificant figures. In the 3rd Army, according to Patton's record, for three corps of 12, then 14, divisions, between March 22 and May 8,1945, they amounted to 2,160 killed, 8,143 wounded, and 644 missing, under 11,000 in all, compared with nearly 15,000 evacuated because of sickness and accidental injury.

On the left of the 12th Army Group, the American 9th Army, straddling the Autobahn from Cologne to Frankfurt-am-Oder to the south of Berlin, thrust towards Hannover, which it took on April 10, and three days later reached Wolmirstedt on the left bank of the Elbe, 85 miles further east. With the capture of Barby, slightly upstream of Magdeburg, it established a first bridgehead on the right bank of the river, thus putting its 83rd Division (Major-General R. C. Macon) some 75 miles from the New

Chancellery. But then it turned instead towards Dessau and made contact there with the 6th Armoured Division (Major-General G. W. Read), which was moving ahead of the 1st Army.

The 1st Army had crossed the Weser at Münden and driven across Thuringia on a line linking Göttingen, Nordhausen, and Eisleben, covering nearly 80 miles between April 8 and 12. As has been mentioned above, it was its left flank that made contact with the 9th Army's right. This pincer movement cut off the retreat of the German 11th Army, which had stayed in the Harz mountains as ordered. To clear a way through for withdrawal, O.K.W. sent the "Clausewitz" Panzer Division to the rescue. It attacked at the junction between the 21st and 12th Army Groups and inflicted some damage on the 9th Army. But having got 35 to 40 miles from its point of departure, in the region of Braunschweig, it too was enveloped and annihilated. The same fate struck the 11th Army, falling almost to a man into Allied hands.

In the centre of the 1st Army, VIII Corps, after reaching the Elbe, managed to establish a bridgehead at Wittenberg, while to its right, VII Corps took Halle and Leipzig on April 14. The capture of Leipzig was a combined effort with the 9th Armoured Division, from the 3rd Army. In accordance with his instructions, General Hodges waited for some days on the Mulde, and it was only on April 26 at Torgau that he met up with Colonel-General Zhadov, commanding he Soviet 5th Guards Army. In the course of this rapid advance the 1st Army came across 300 tons of Wilhelmstrasse archives deposited in various places in the Harz. At Nordhausen, it occupied the vast underground factories where most of the V-1 and V-2 missiles were manufactured.

On March 30 the impetuous Patton was on the Werra and the Fulda. On April 12, the 3rd Army, changing its direction from north-east to east, crossed the Saale at Naumburg, Jena, and Saalfeld, having broken the last serious resistance offered by the enemy at Mühlhausen in Thuringia. And on April 7 the 3rd Army took the 400,000th prisoner since its campaign opened. On the 21st following, XX Corps reached Saxony and the vicinity of Chemnitz, VIII Corps reached a point beyond Plauen, while XII Corps, changing course from east to south-east, had got well beyond Bayreuth in Bavaria. This was the last exploit by Manton S. Eddy who suffered a heart attack and had to hand over his corps to Major-General Stafford LeRoy Irwin. If the 1st Army had captured the Wilhelmstrasse archives, the 3rd discovered the last reserves of the Reichsbank, composed of gold bars worth 500,000,000 francs, small quantities of French, Belgian, and Norwegian currency and 3,000,000,000 marks in notes.

An ultimate regrouping by Bradley switched VIII Corps from Patton's command to Hodges's, and the progressive collapse of Army Group "B" permitted III and V Corps to be switched to the 3rd Army. Thus strengthened, it was given the assignment of supporting the activities of the 7th Army in Bavaria and upper Austria; specifically, to prevent the enemy establishing himself in the "national redoubt" zone. Patton advanced with all speed, and on the day of the surrender he had pushed his XII Corps to a point ten miles below Linz on the Austrian Danube, and his III Corps, whose command had been taken over by Major-General James A. Van Fleet, as far as Rosenheim at the foot of the Bavarian Alps. On May 2, his 13th Armoured Division (Major-General

Millikin) crossed the Inn at Braunau, birthplace of Adolf Hitler, who had just committed suicide in his bunker in the Berlin Chancellery.

Patton would have liked to complete his triumph by maintaining the drive of V (Major-General Clarence R. Huebner) and XII Corps as far as Prague. But on May 6, Eisenhower sent him categorical instructions via Bradley not to go beyond the Ceske Budejovice–Plzen–Karlovy Vary line in Czechoslovakia which he had reached. By this action, the Supreme Allied Commander, who had consulted Marshal Antonov, Stalin's Chief-of-Staff, on the matter, yielded to the objections such an operation raised in the Soviet camp. In any event, the American 3rd Army met the spearhead of the 3rd Ukrainian Front, which had come up the Danube from Vienna, at Linz.

## Montgomery drives for Lübeck

Montgomery's main task now was to push through to Lübeck and cut off the German forces occupying Norway and Denmark. For this purpose, he disposed of the British 2nd Army and the Canadian 1st Army, comprising five corps of 16 divisions (six of them armoured). Before him in Holland he found the German 25th Army, of which General von Blumentritt had just assumed command, and the debris of the 1st Parachute Army. This debilitated force had been put under the overall command of Field-Marshal Busch, who had been placed at the head of a Northern Defence Zone, to include the Netherlands, north-west Germany, Denmark, and Norway. Weakness in numbers and matériel was, however, to some extent offset by the fact that tracts

*Struthof concentration camp, France.*

of bog and the otherwise marshy nature of the ground kept the tanks to the main roads.

Having captured Münster, the key to Westphalia, General Dempsey, commanding the British 2nd Army, pushed forward his XXX Corps in the direction of Bremen, XII Corps towards Hamburg, and VIII Corps towards Lübeck.

On the right, VIII Corps (Lieutenant-General Sir Evelyn H. Barker) was momentarily delayed by the "Clausewitz" Panzer Division's counter-attack which, as has been mentioned above, was aimed at the point of contact of the 21st and 12th Army Groups. Nonetheless, VIII Corps reached the Elbe opposite Lauenburg on April 19. Here, Montgomery, anxious to move

with all possible speed, requested support from Eisenhower and was given the U.S. XVIII Airborne Corps (8th Division, 5th and 7th Armoured Divisions, and the U.S. 82nd Airborne and British 6th Airborne Divisions). On April 29–30, British and Americans under cover provided by the first R.A.F. jet fighters, Gloster Meteors, forced the Elbe. On May 2, 11th Armoured Division (Major-General Roberts), which was the spearhead of the British VIII Corps, occupied Lübeck and the 6th Airborne Division entered Wismar, 28 miles further east, six hours ahead of Marshal Rokossovsky's leading patrols.

## Hamburg and Bremen taken

XII Corps (Lieutenant-General Ritchie) had to sustain one

*The fall of Berlin.*

last challenge on April 6 when crossing the Aller, a tributary on the right bank of the Weser. Afterwards, it took advantage of the bridgehead won on the Elbe by VIII Corps and closed in on Hamburg. On May 2, Lieutenant-General Wolz surrendered the ruins of the great Hanseatic port. Two days later, the 7th Armoured Division (Major-General Lyne) captured intact a bridge over the Kiel Canal at Eckernförde. Ritchie, who was within 35 miles of the town of Flensburg, where Grand-Admiral Dönitz had recently taken over the responsibilities of head of state, had brilliantly avenged the defeat inflicted on him at Tobruk.

In their drive on Bremen, Sir Brian Horrocks and his XXX Corps were held up by a great deal of destruction, and met with altogether fiercer resistance. Before Lingen, what was left of the 7th Parachute Division carried through a hand-to-hand counter-attack with frenetic "Heil Hitler" battle cries.

The 2nd Kriegsmarine Division showed the same aggressive spirit in defence, and it needed a pincer movement staged by three divisions to bring about the fall of Bremen on April 26. A few hours before the cease-fire, the Guards Armoured Division occupied Cuxhaven at the mouth of the Elbe.

## Canadians in Holland

On April 1, General Crerar, commanding the Canadian 1st Army, recovered his II Corps, reinforced by the British 49th Division, thus bringing his divisions up to six. His mission was twofold: to drive between the Weser and the Zuiderzee with the British XXX Corps in the general direction of Wilhelmshaven and Emden; and to liberate the Dutch provinces still occupied by the enemy. The Canadian II Corps (Lieutenant-General Simonds), which had taken part in the crossing of the Rhine, fulfilled the first of these missions. On April 6, it liberated Zutphen and Almelo, and four days later Groningen and Leeuwarden. In this fine action, it was greatly helped by Dutch resistance while the French 2nd and 3rd Parachute Regiments dropped in the area of Assem and Meppel to open a way for it over the Orange Canal. On German territory, however, General Straube's II Parachute Corps put up a desperate fight, and Crerar had to call on Montgomery for help from the Polish 1st Armoured Division, the Canadian 5th Armoured Division, and the British 3rd Division. With this shot of new blood, the Canadian II Corps accelerated its advance and on May 5, 1945, General Maczek's Polish 1st Armoured Division was within nine miles of Wilhelmshaven, and the Canadian 5th Armoured Division on the outskirts of Emden.

The Canadian I Corps (Lieutenant-General C. Foulkes) took Arnhem by an outflanking movement and three days later reached the Zuiderzee at Harderwijk. The Germans responded to this attack by opening the sea-dykes, and Crerar, who was concerned to spare the Dutch countryside the ravages of flooding, agreed to a cease-fire with General von Blumentritt, stipulating in exchange that British and American aircraft be given free passage to provide the Dutch population with food and medical supplies. This dual operation cost the Canadian 1st Army 367 officers and 5,147 N.C.O.s and other ranks killed, wounded, and missing.

## Last German high command change

While Field-Marshal Busch had been entrusted with the command of a "Northern Defence Zone", Kesselring was called upon to lead a "Southern Defence Zone" which included the German forces fighting between the Main and the Swiss frontier. So during the final phase of the campaign he found himself facing General Devers, whose 6th Army Group numbered 20 divisions on March 30, 1945, and 22 (13 American and nine French) the following May 8.

## Advance to Berchtesgaden

The task of Lieutenant-General Patch and the American 7th Army was to cross the Rhine upstream of the 3rd Army, then having gained enough ground to the east, turn down towards Munich and make an assault on the "national redoubt", where, according to Eisenhower's Intelligence, Hitler would seek ultimate refuge. On March 26, XV Corps of the American 7th Army managed without much trouble to cross the Rhine at Gernsheim below Worms. Patch exploited this success by taking Michelstadt then, turning south, he took Mannheim and Heidelberg on March 30. On April 5, having moved up the Neckar as far as Heilbronn, he captured Würzburg in the Main valley. With his left as spearhead, he hurled his forces in the direction Schweinfurt–Bamberg–Nuremberg and on April 19, after some violent fighting, ended all resistance in Munich. With its right wing in contact with the French 1st Army in the Stuttgart area, and the left in touch with the American 3rd, the 7th Army moved in a south-easterly direction. On April 25, it crossed the Danube on an 80 mile front, capturing on the way what was left of XIII Corps with its commanding officer, Lieutenant-General Count d'Oriola.

From that moment German resistance in Bavaria collapsed. On May 2, the American XV Corps occupied Munich. Two days later, the French 2nd Armoured Division, once more free for assignment with the Royan pocket liquidated, scaled the slopes of the Obersalzberg and occupied the Berghof, from which Reichsmarschall Hermann Göring had just fled. On the same day, the American 3rd Division, which had sped through Innsbruck, crossed the Brenner Pass and met up with the 88th Division of the American 5th Army at Vipiteno. On May 5, General Schulz, last commander of Army Group "G", avoiding capture by the French, surrendered at General Jacob L. Devers's H.Q.

## Victory in Europe

Hitler dismissed Guderian and appointed Colonel-General H. Krebs as his successor on March 28, 1945. Army Group "Vistula" was charged with the defence of Berlin. The German 9th Army with 12 divisions had the task of barring the way to Berlin.

Marshal Zhukov's 1st Belorussian Front was tasked with taking Berlin. On his left Marshal Konev was to force the Neisse and exploit his victory along the Bautzen-Dresden axis.

At 0400 hours on April 16 the attack started, but made slow progress. By April 19, however, the German 9th Army disintegrated. Hitler called the German 12th Army out of the Western Front to move on Berlin. Meanwhile the Red Army fired 25,600 tons of shells onto the city.

*Alfred Jodl, Chief of German general staff signs surrender document, Rheims, France, 7 May 1945.*

Hitler dismissed Hermann Goring and Heinrich Himmler from the Party, married Eva Braun, made his will and committed suicide on April 30. On May 2, 1945, Berlin surrendered. On May 3 on Lunenburg Heath the German Army of the North offered to surrender to Montgomery. The final surrender on May 4 limited the forces surrendering to those opposing 21st Army Group. At Rheims on May 7, 1945 Eisenhower received a German delegation that signed a surrender document. On May 8, the final act of the Wehrmacht's and Third Reich's unconditional surrender was signed in Berlin.

# CHRONOLOGY OF WORLD WAR II

| | 1938 |
|---|---|
| March 11 | Anschluss — German annexation of Austria. |
| September 29 | Munich Agreement signed. |
| October 5 | Germany occupies Sudetenland. |

| | 1939 |
|---|---|
| March 14 | Slovakia declares its independence. |
| March 31 | Britain and France give guarantee to Poland. |
| April 7 | Italy invades Albania. |
| May 22 | Germany and Italy sign Pact of Steel. |
| August 23 | Molotov-Ribbentrop pact signed between Germany and the Soviet Union. |
| September 1 | Germany invades Poland. |
| September 1 | Britain and France declare war on Germany. |
| September 17 | Soviet Union invades Poland. |
| November 30 | Soviet Union at war with Finland. |

| | 1940 |
|---|---|
| March 12 | War between Soviet Union and Finland ends. |
| April 9 | Germany invades Norway and Denmark. |
| April 14 | Allied troops land in Norway. |
| May 10 | Fall Gelb, the offensive in the West, is launched by Germany. |
| May 10 | Churchill becomes Prime Minister of Great Britain. |
| May 14 | Dutch Army surrenders. |
| May 26 | Beginning of evacuation of Dunkirk. |
| May 28 | Belgium surrenders. |
| June 2 | Allies withdraw from Norway. |
| June 4 | Dunkirk evacuation complete. |
| June 10 | Italy declares war on Britain and France. |
| June 14 | Germans enter Paris. |
| June 21 | Italy launches offensive against France. |
| June 22 | France and Germany sign armistice. |
| June 24 | France and Italy sign armistice. |
| July 3 | Royal Navy attacks French fleet at Mers el Kebir. |
| July 10 | Beginning of the Battle of Britain. |
| September 17 | Operation Sealion (the invasion of England) postponed by Hitler. |
| September 21 | Italy and Germany sign Tripartite Pact. |
| September 27 | Japan signs Tripartite Pact. |
| November 20 | Hungary signs Tripartite Pact. |
| November 22 | Romania signs Tripartite Pact. |
| November 23 | Slovakia signs Tripartite Pact. |

| | 1941 |
|---|---|
| January 19 | British launch East African campaign offensive. |
| January 22 | Australian troops take Tobruk. |
| February 6 | British capture Benghazi. |
| February 11 | Rommel arrives in Libya. |

| | |
|---|---|
| **March 25** | Yugoslavia signs Tripartite Pact. |
| **March 27** | Yugoslavia leaves Tripartite Pact after coup d'etat. |
| **March 28** | Successful British naval action against Italians off Cape Matapan. |
| **April 6–8** | Axis forces invade Yugoslavia and Greece. |
| **April 11** | U.S.A. extends its naval neutrality patrols. |
| **April 13** | Belgrade falls to Axis forces. |
| **April 14** | Yugoslav forces surrender. |
| **April 22** | Greek First Army surrenders at Metsovan Pass. |
| **May 16** | Italians surrender to British at Amba Alagi. |
| **May 20** | Germans land on Crete. |
| **May 24** | H.M.S. Hood sunk by Bismarck. |
| **May 27** | Bismarck sunk by Royal Navy. |
| **June 1** | British withdraw from Crete. |
| **June 2** | Germany launches Operation Barbarossa against the Soviet Union. |
| **July 27** | Japanese troops invade French Indo-China. |
| **September 19** | Germans capture Kiev. |
| **September 28** | Three-power Conference in Moscow. |
| **December 6** | Britain declares war on Finland, Hungary and Rumania. |
| **December 7** | Japanese attack Pearl Harbor. |
| **December 8** | U.S.A. and Britain declare war on Japan. |
| **December 8** | Japanese invade Malaya and Thailand. |
| **December 11** | Germany and Italy declare war on the U.S.A. |
| **December 14** | Japanese begin invasion of Burma. |
| **December 25** | Japanese take Hong Kong. |
| **1942** | |
| **February 15** | Japanese troops capture Singapore from British. |
| **February 27** | Battle of the Java Sea. |
| **February 28** | Japanese invade Java. |
| **March 8** | Japanese invade New Guinea. |
| **March 17** | General MacArthur appointed to command South-West Pacific. |
| **April 9** | U.S. troops surrender in Bataan. |
| **April 16** | George Cross awarded to Island of Malta by H.R.H. King George VI. |
| **April 26** | Anglo-Soviet Treaty signed. |
| **May 6** | Japanese take Corregidor. |
| **May 7** | Battle of the Coral Sea. |
| **May 20** | British troops withdraw from Burma. |
| **May 26** | Rommel's Afrika Korps attack British at Gazala. |
| **May 30** | Royal Air Force launches first thousand-bomber raid on Germany. |
| **June 4** | Battle of Midway. |
| **June 21** | Rommel's Afrika Korps take Tobruk. |
| **July 1** | Sevastopol taken by Germans. |
| **July 1** | First Battle of El Alamein. |
| **August 7** | U.S. troops land on Guadalcanal. |
| **August 11** | PEDESTAL convoy arrives in Malta. |
| **August 19** | Raid on Dieppe. |

| | |
|---|---|
| **August 31** | Battle of Alam Halfa. |
| **October 24** | Second Battle of El Alamein. |
| **November 8** | Operation TORCH landings in North Africa. |
| **November 11** | Germans and Italians occupy Vichy France. |
| **November 27** | French fleet scuttled at Toulon. |
| **1943** | |
| **January 14–24** | Allied Conference at Casablanca. |
| **January 23** | British troops take Tripoli. |
| **February 2** | Germans surrender at Stalingrad. |
| **February 8** | Red Army captures Kursk. |
| **February 13** | Chindits launch first operation into Burma. |
| **February 19** | Battle for the Kasserine Pass. |
| **April 19** | First Warsaw rising. |
| **April 19** | Bermuda Conference. |
| **May 11–25** | TRIDENT conference in Washington. |
| **May 13** | Axis forces surrender in North Africa. |
| **May 16** | Royal Air Force "Dambuster" raid on Mohne and Eder dams. |
| **May 24** | U-boats withdraw from North Atlantic. |
| **July 5** | Battle of Kursk. |
| **July 10** | Allies land in Sicily. |
| **July 25** | Mussolini resigns. |
| **September 3** | Allies land on Italian mainland. |
| **September 8** | Surrender of Italy announced. |
| **September 9** | Allies land at Salerno. |
| **September 10** | Germans occupy Rome and Northern Italy. |
| **October 13** | Italy declares war on Germany. |
| **November 6** | Red Army captures Kiev. |
| **November** | First Allied conference in Cairo. 23–26 |
| **November 28–December 1** | Allied conference in Teheran. |
| **December 3–7** | Second Allied conference in Cairo. |
| **December 24** | General Eisenhower promoted to supreme commander for OVERLORD, the Normandy landings. |
| **1944** | |
| **January 22** | Allies land at Anzio. |
| **January 27** | Red Army raises Siege of Leningrad. |
| **January 31** | U.S. forces land on Marshall Islands. |
| **February 1** | Battle for Monte Cassino begins. |
| **March 2** | Second Chindit operation into Burma. |
| **May 11** | Fourth Battle of Monte Cassino. |
| **June 4** | U.S. troops enter Rome. |
| **June 6** | Operation OVERLORD — Allied landings in Normandy. |
| **June 19** | Battle of the Philippine Sea. |
| **July 1** | Breton Woods conference. |
| **July 20** | Failed attempt to assassinate Hitler — July Bomb plot. |
| **August 1** | Second Warsaw rising. |
| **August 4** | Allied troops enter Florence. |

| | |
|---|---|
| **August 15** | Operation DRAGOON — Allied landings in southern France. |
| **August 25** | Germans in Paris surrender. |
| **September 4** | British troops capture Antwerp. |
| **September** | OCTAGON — Allied conference at Quebec. 12–16 |
| **September 17** | Operation MARKET GARDEN at Arnhem. |
| **September 21** | Dumbarton Oaks conference. |
| **October 14** | British enter Athens. |
| **October 23** | De Gaulle recognised by Britain and U.S.A. as head of French Provisional Government. |
| **October 24** | Battle of Leyte Gulf. |
| **December 16** | Germans launch campaign in the Ardennes. |
| **1945** | |
| **January 4–13** | Japanese Kamikaze planes sink 17 U.S. ships and damage 50 more. |
| **January 14** | Red Army advances into East Prussia. |
| **January 17** | Red Army takes Warsaw. |
| **January 30–February 3** | First ARGONAUT Allied conference at Malta. |
| **February 4–11** | Second ARGONAUT Allied conference at Malta. |
| **February 6** | Allies clear Colmar pocket. |
| **February 19** | U.S. forces land on Iwo Jima. |
| **February 26** | U.S. 9th Army reaches Rhine. |
| **March 7** | U.S. 3rd Army crosses Rhine at Remagen Bridge. |
| **March 20** | British capture Mandalay. |
| **March 30** | Red Army enters Austria. |
| **April 1** | U.S. First and Ninth Armies encircle the Ruhr. |
| **April 1** | U.S. forces land on Okinawa. |
| **April 12** | President Roosevelt dies and Truman becomes president. |
| **April 13** | Red Army takes Vienna. |
| **April 25** | U.S. and Soviet forces meet at Torgau. |
| **April 28** | Mussolini shot by partisans. |
| **April 29** | Germans sign surrender terms for troops in Italy. |
| **April 30** | Hitler commits suicide. |
| **May 2** | Red Army takes Berlin. |
| **May 3** | British enter Rangoon. |
| **May 4** | German forces in the Netherlands, northern Germany and Denmark surrender to General Montgomery on Luneburg Heath. |
| **May 5** | Germans in Norway surrender. |
| **May 7** | General Alfred Jodl signs unconditional surrender of Germany at Reims, to take effect on May 9. |
| **May 8** | Victory in Europe Day. |
| **May 10** | Red Army takes Prague. |
| **July 17–August 2** | Allied TERMINAL conference held in Potsdam. |
| **July 26** | Winston Churchill resigns after being defeated in the general election. Clement Attlee becomes Prime Minister of Great Britain. |
| **August 6** | Atomic bomb dropped on Hiroshima. |
| **August 8** | Soviet Union declares war on Japan. |
| **August 9** | Atomic bomb dropped on Nagasaki. |
| **August 14** | Unconditional surrender of Japanese forces announced by Emperor Hirohito. |
| **August 15** | Victory in Japan Day. |
| **September 2** | Japanese sign surrender aboard U.S.S. Missouri in Tokyo Bay. |